Festival Images for Today

Festival Images for Today

CARLO PIETZNER

Published in the United States by
Camphill Publications, USA
Box 300A, R.D. 1, Glenmoore, PA 19343

In cooperation with
Anthroposophic Press
RR 4 Box 94 A-1, Hudson, NY 12534

Library of Congress Cataloging-in-Publication Data

Pietzner, Carlo, 1915-1986
Festival Images for Today

Bibliography: p.
1. Cultural—Religion
2. Anthroposophy. I. Title

ISBN 0-88010-376-0

Cover design by Cornelius M. Pietzner
Painting by Carlo Pietzner

Printed in the United States of America

Table of Contents

Introduction

Festivals, like art, are a creation of man which reaches into the realm of the spirit. Like art, the celebration of festivals "produces" something, if I can use that word, which can inspire and transform us. Like art, festivals are for everyone, not just the few and, like art, the ability to celebrate festivals can be a measure of the strength, vitality and inner dynamic of a person, community or culture.

Festivals contain and imply something essential, and have always been a part of the stream of human evolution. Moments of uplifted consciousness in which a people or culture combine their efforts to celebrate, for whatever reason, belong to the basic structure of life itself. Not to acknowledge the reality and necessity of festivals is to deprive oneself of participating in one of the deepest rhythms of life. Today, with a surfeit of material convenience surrounding every aspect of our outer lives, we can nevertheless experience a profound bankruptcy in the moral tapestry and imagination of our social life. It is through the forces of imagination, inspiration and intuition that we connect ourselves to those spheres of our existence which inform and inspire the life of festivals. Particularly in the west, superficial images and phantoms of all kinds have been imbedded into our collective and individual imagination by mass media and popular culture to such an extent

that our own inner resources have dried up and shriv-
eled. Even more tragically the awareness of our own
impoverishment and lack of creativity has become
dull and inactive. The constant buzz and whine of
consumer technology through digital means (like
video, t.v., movies, c.d interactive, etc.), coupled with
the popular culture of Hollywood and science fiction
has supplanted the more subtle, basic and fundamental struggle to create imaginations out of the language and illumination of our own inner life. In
many ways we have become a literal-minded culture,
compromising the indirection of metaphor for the
gratification of instant reality.

Thus, it is even more imperative to dwell and lin-
ger on what is almost lost, with the attempt to regain
our sense for the sacred, for the unusual (*not* the bi-
zarre) for the holy and ephemeral which is such an
important part of our lives and which belongs so es-
sentially to the continuing attempt to create a modern and relevant festival celebration.

The many and ongoing attempts to create festivals out of the background of spiritual science has
been a great practicing ground through which a pan-
oply of activities and artistic resources can be synthe-
sized and coordinated. In countless Waldorf schools,
curative and social therapeutic settings, bio-dynamic
farms and private dwellings the punctuation of festival celebrations has created a deliberate signature of
the rhythms of life, in which drama and pageantry,
puppetry and eurythmy, speech and song can meld
into a triumphant and joyous synchronization. Both
the major and less known festivals are lifted into artistic and social consciousness, articulating a fine and
delicate contour to the passing of seasons.

This book is a compendium of lectures given by Carlo Pietzner to different listeners over many years. Always a community moment, the celebration of the festivals within Camphill, whether large or small, has been, and continues to be, a time of coming together, to assess, ponder and reflect. Carlo's lectures during such times were occasions to pause and consider national or world events through the image or lens of a particular festival. Conversely, in some of these lectures, the particular festival itself was to be highlighted and considered through the lens of the present time and one or another phenomenon of note.

In many instances the lectures were given to a group of Camphill villagers or coworkers, sometimes at the occasion of a conference or workshop around a specific community festival theme—long a tradition in many Camphill centers. We have certainly retained the basic "feel" of these lectures, and, as Carlo was speaking to audiences he knew well, the style in most instances is not formal. Style was important to Carlo—important because he wished to convey important things regardless of whether his listeners were mentally handicapped or well-seasoned anthroposophists. Thus we have retained many personal references and idiomatic phrases. Indeed, in some areas both the content and the style are quite intimate.

For many years Carlo's lectures were issued in single editions and sold separately in anthroposophical outlets in many parts of the world. Over time this method proved unsatisfactory and we have therefore arranged approximately 60-75 lectures into topical themes to be published in a series of books. This edition is the first of the series, containing fourteen lectures on a diverse range of images connected to the festivals.

Some of the current titles have been altered from the original single issues to clarify meaning and content. It is difficult to summarize the content of any individual lecture, as many of the images and concepts which Carlo attempted to bring to life are subtle and tenuous. As a charismatic speaker the mood of a lecture could itself advance a nuance and confirm meaning. Reading parts of a lecture may not recreate the stream or flow which an oral rendering could impart. In his lecturing, for instance, he would often develop a theme in response to a question or issue, or out of circumstances happening on that day—the attempt to sculpt his thoughts even as he spoke was almost a palpable experience for those who attended his presentations. Thus, where possible, it could be recommended to read an entire lecture or more "in one sitting".

A word still about the cover: As an artist, Carlo's work took many forms. His chief love was painting. He was trained as a painter, and in the last third of his life was able to return with greater concentration to his painting. He provided many Camphill centers, as well as countless friends, with a wonderful portfolio of sketches, pastels, acrylics and large oils. One of these we have chosen for this cover related as it is to the Michaelmas season.

This project has been aided by several people. Jean Hall helped with typing, the Camphill Foundation through the Carlo Pietzner Fund facilitated financial support, and Christl Bender provided invaluable assistance in proofing and researching often obscure references, and she therefore gets special thanks.

If this volume can serve to inspire a deeper imagination regarding the rhythms, nature and meaning of the festivals or confirm perhaps tentative and searching thoughts and feelings it will have achieved' its purpose.

— Cornelius M. Pietzner
St. John's 1993

On the Quest for Image and Reality in Relation to Death and the Ego

August, 1969, Spring Valley, NY

Dear Friends:

Somebody said to me yesterday evening that I spoke about an old problem[1] and this is, of course, utterly true. I will continue to speak about an old problem this morning, and I will even do something that is not thought to be quite proper nowadays; I will quote a great deal from Rudolf Steiner. I am one of those who believes that there are times in which it is good for us to be reminded what "der Doktor hat gesagt." I still like to try to live in some of his words and indications as one of the great orientating sources to which we all can turn today.

I would like also to say that one of the reasons why I felt I should speak about image and reality has to do

---

1. The question of Image and Reality was addressed. However extensive references were made to the moon landing and its implications—which had occurred roughly a week earlier and we have therefore chosen not to reprint that lecture.

with the events of the moon landing. It has to do with
the fact that we can not yet assess what it means that
one of the most powerful images that ruled the minds
of men over millennia, the moon, has, so to speak,
been taken hold of, has been gripped by what pre-
tends to be the only reality. The moon is the holy symbol for Islam, and for many, many people the moon
is the image that so often accompanies lovers. It will
never be quite the same anymore. For many their image has been rudely trespassed by this remarkable,
heavy-footed step that we made on its surface. I believe we have to ask ourselves whether the silver sickle
of the moon holding the dark part of the moon in its
cup will now no longer bear the name of Parcival as
we walk on our inner path? We must try to see all this
together as an urgent demand within the confines of
an old problem.

We spoke yesterday about the fact that our consciousness is still a picture-making consciousness. We
have in ourselves, as an accompanying note, the
deep question about the reality of ego-consciousness. Of course, we have self-consciousness. Our consciousness today, compared with the imagery or
picture-consciousness of the past, is incomparably
different. But do we have, and if so in what direction
can we look for, an understanding of an ego-conducted ego-consciousness? We spoke yesterday about
three steps which I quickly want to recall. These inner steps are constantly performed by us, though un-
consciously and by no means within the confines of
an ego-conducted consciousness. These steps are
taking place through the potent power that gives us
our ego-awareness, the power of our memory. We are
confronted with an event, with an occurrence or an

object, and when we relate ourselves to it—or we might also say: when this event relates itself to us—we begin the complicated process of wrapping it up into the tissues of our memory. One moment we have seen or experienced something; the following step already is one step removed from what has seemingly been the reality. We have to remember it and later on, when perhaps after some months we recall it, it seems to us—though strangely further bereft of the immediacy of reality—somehow more real, more meaningful. A careful selection has taken place. Later on, as the third step, we are able to behold, to see this event in the context in which it has actually occurred but which revealed itself only over a much longer period of time as part of our *own* biography. Then, although it has undergone a very definite selective process and is in some ways perhaps different from what actually occurred, it now seems to us infinitely more real. In fact, it has now attained the reality in which it finds a place in what we conceive to be the picture of ourself, in our auto-biography.

Today we want to turn to a different aspect of image-making and having pictures, namely to that which is related to the world and to others and to their effects. The respect which we used to have for the occurrence of an illness, for the process of illness, has given way to hatred against the intruder. It has given way to a totally different attitude, determined by our consciousness, concerning the place of illness in our lives. This must be seen against the most fundamental background of the determining factors for most of our consciousness today—our relationship to death and the increasing fear of death—appearing as a pathologically deteriorating relationship of millions of people to death. When illness is regarded as an intruder, when death is regarded as the threatening final end, we have to confess that it is the way we look at all this, the image which we have of ourselves, which makes such relationships possible.

It is more than well known that this image we have of ourselves is continuously becoming more unreal, is deteriorating. The questions as to who one is, what it is when one becomes ill, how one can relate oneself to death, are increasingly unsolved. They are creating the most difficult tensions, illnesses, confusions. With this goes the fact that the disintegration of a well-defined image of ourselves (as we thought we had in even the more recent past) is simply no longer applicable. Where it is retained through pressures in the social order, coercion of class distinctions and by innumerable other means we know that all this belongs to the past. The revolt of the younger generations properly and rightly begins to undermine it.

Their revolt is against all that is a mask instead of an image. Their revolt against the so-called establishment and all that goes with it, the revolt also against what is supposed to be the risk of disease, against our carefully antiseptic world, all this has to come about. In a world in which, from the cradle to the grave, one wants to eliminate germs, there must arise fanatics against dirt. One of the most important symptoms is the fear of death that has become totally anonymous. Death is no longer understandable within some kind of world-order and has become faceless. Of course, for a long time, death has played the role of the final end of the personality. But it is only since ancient Greece—and then not for the majority of people— that it has begun to have this kind of place in Western civilizations. Today we cannot deny the fact once expressed by Rudolf Steiner in the one shattering sentence: The only reality on earth is death[1]. Today we are only acknowledging a fact that has prepared itself over the centuries and millennia. But we have not yet begun to investigate what this reality of death can mean for us. It seems that the only truly real experience we can have is death. If death is the only experience which we can have that is of reality, then we must learn to regard death as if it were a fountain, a fountain as one previously spoke about the fountain of life. We have to learn what droplets from this fountain of death we can use to infuse all our other possibilities of existence with reality. Thus we have to turn toward the reality of death, which means—turning *towards* death instead of turning away from it.

One of the most consistent experiences of psychiatrists, most expertly described by Rollo May[2], is that pathological conditions of the soul occur, or are aggravated, by turning away from the origin of these difficulties—for instance, loneliness. But if one walks consciously and with acceptance toward loneliness it begins to reveal itself as a quality, a value. This is much more difficult to do with death. To turn towards death means to face into a different direction. In this moment, when we turn toward death or think without abhorrence about death, we turn toward love. We begin to wonder about the saying, or the hope, that love triumphs over death. But we would

---

1. "Das Geheimnis des Todes"—Stuttgart, Nov. 22, 1915—not published in English.
2. Rollo May is one of the original founders of the School of Existential Psychotherapy. Author of *"Man's Search for Himself"*, *"Love and Will"* (quoted here) and other books.

have to learn this with the life blood of reality. We are very far from this today. I would like to quote from Rollo May: "There is more to the relationship between death and love; our obsession with sex covers up our fear of death. We lack the belief in immortality that armored our ancestors and we also lack any widely agreed upon purpose of life. Consequently the awareness of death is widely repressed in our day, but none of us can fail to be aware of the tremendous preoccupation with sex in our humor, our drama and our economic life, even our television commercials. An obsession drains off anxiety from some other area and prevents us from confronting something distasteful. What would we have to see if we could cut through our obsession about sex? That we must die. The clamor of sex drowns out the ever awaiting presence of death"[1]. Another psychiatrist has said that one must doubt our capacity to love passionately if we would not be so imbued with the knowledge that we and the other one must die.

In this moment one can divine an extraordinarily important relationship which yet is intimately near to us. This relates to our identity for which we search as so many people do in our time. So many feel they don't have any identity. Where is it? The identity of each person in life must be paralleled, if it is to be a total identity, by his identity in death. Perhaps the most contemporary prayer would be to say "Lord, give me my own death." The feeling of millions of people is that their life, so important as a signature of something undefinable, is accidental. This is today reinforced with a tremendous, overpowering cruelty, by

---

1. See above: *"Love and Will"*.

the anonymity of death and by the seemingly accidental way in which death occurs. We are indoctrinated by every newspaper, every broadcast and television program by the recital of accidents which occur. In fact our communications media would go out of business if people would not die spectacularly. This is constantly impressed upon us; not only that people die but how accidentally they die.

Hundreds of thousands of people feel that they are helpless to do anything about all this. But we *can* do something. This something lies in the fact that we can make images of ourselves and of other people. To make true images of ourselves and the people with whom we meet is probably the most crucial need of all, whether it is reflected in the experiences of a family, or of a group of people both at work and play, or of a community, or of a spiritually striving society, whatever it may be. The image which we have of ourselves in relationship to others and they of us is crucial for the effect any of these relationships will have on the world. We know that to make an image of ourselves begins in earliest infancy. We gain an image of our own body; we grasp our Gestalt in the very first movements in childhood when we began to have sense-experiences. These first experiences echo the first outlines of an image. They belong to the most vital for the appropriate functioning of a normal person later on. And where they do not take place, either through a psychological or physical disturbance, the results, manifesting perhaps in the very movements of such a person, may remind you of the moon-walker. Such a person has not found his relationship to the earthly forces with which he has to deal. But these first important and fundamental experiences, reinforced by the vital periods of interruption that occur through the child's sleep, lead on to ever more complicated and at least semi-conscious image-experiences of oneself. To these are added elements of the gradually arriving image beamed to us by the reactions of our peers, by the reactions of other people to us. Our dependence on these reactions has barely begun to be properly evaluated.

The dean of one of the California universities has recently said: "In the age of T.V., image is more important than substance and reality." It is a very interesting statement! What he meant was that if he is presented with an appropriate image by the media, that would be more important than whether there was a real substance behind it. How deeply true this is! But it is not only true in this way. Do we know to what extent we can imprison each other in the image which we hold of one another? Do we know to what extent, particularly in long-term relationships, the image that two people have of each other can become like a husk within which the reality of their relationship begins to dry out? Is it not one of the most potent undermining factors of marriage that the freshness of discovery, as it is blunted by usage, by intimacy, dries up? What is left is the husk of quickly-sketched and long-practiced images one has of one another. Do we not frequently practice this cutting down of each other to that size of an image which we can realistically assume will be accepted by most people? Do we not hold back people in their positions, in their attempts, sometimes even beyond the pattern their predecessors have created and more than they are capable of achieving by themselves? If I am so emphatic about this, it is because it is related to another quality which helped us greatly in the past and which has ceased to be helpful.

What is a mask now was once upon a time what could be called 'ein Leitbild'—a guiding image, according to which people were able to live. The king—as an image; the courtier, the farmer, the miller—but also, gradually, in our societies the successful banker, the established father, images that played into the lives of millions of people as types, as archetypal images according to which man directed his conduct. In this he felt himself to a certain extent defined, yet today we have lost much of the meaning of this.

Even though people are ever more confused about their identity, an overriding longing is working in people, young and old, to be *themselves*, though we don't know what or who that is. Who am I,—because I am and must be I, and not somebody else. "I" am not a professional mantle, nor the craftsman's mantle, nor the father's mantle, nor the daughter's or son's mantle—*I* must be I. But never was there less certainty of what this 'I' is. But perhaps this is so because for the first time our little 'I', even if only as a question, has really now appeared upon the earth within the consciousness of ordinary man.

Dear friends, parallel with this, as a consequence, is the growing certainty that there must be repeated earth lives. We cannot possibly equate who we feel we must be with the ridiculous thing that we are! We can no longer accept the inconsolable fact that for so long and still for a good long time to come we are only that unsatisfactory, limited being, known to us and others in its limited appearance, which does some very limited, all too earthly deeds.

What we call today Mr. So and So, Mrs. So and So is an image. While it signifies a certain outline of characteristics, possibilities, desires, wishes, in our most important moments we know that that isn't me, that can't be all. But almost immediately when we have felt this, when we have looked behind the curtain, we quickly close it again and become terribly engaged in ourselves, overly engaged. We are frightened that there is something else behind the curtain about which we have really no concept.

It is important to mention this—in relationship to death. In death it doesn't work any more as it works for us while we are alive—when we relate ourselves to people with whom we were deeply and inwardly connected and who have died. It can be a tremendous experience—even if only momentarily—to feel the dead in reality, as spiritually existent beings. If one tries to relate oneself to them with warm, deeply related memory-images, if one gathers up within oneself, so to speak, all these ingredients, one may begin to notice new and different characteristics of our experiences with those who have died. These are different from experiences we were accustomed to have while they were alive. Those images we used to have begin to drop away. In a sense this is already reflected in many of the rites which are held at a funeral when sometimes people who couldn't find a good word for somebody while he was alive, but who has died suddenly, now begin to praise this poor chap. The attitude that after death one can and should only say the best things about a person is in a crude sense reflecting this. But something more subtle occurs. There is a definite difference which one can quite concretely experience with regard to the kind of memory which one has of the dead. It is not the same kind of memory we have for everything else, be it a person who is still alive, or an event or an object. It is not a memory in which the same thing happens as it happens with everything else. No, it can occur that in our memory of someone who has died we are rebutted by the overwhelming reality and presence of that being. We are sometimes even corrected in the changes occurring in our memory.

In a lecture called "Das Geheimmis des Todes"[1], (Stuttgart, November 22, 1915), Rudolf Steiner speaks about this in the following way: "What does it actually mean for the whole of reality *[for the whole of reality!]* when on a day of memory for the dead the souls of men who live here on earth go to the graves or unite themselves in their thoughts with the dead? What does it mean when we on such a memory day create for ourselves hours of memories for the dead; when we, for instance, read to them, when we do something in order to unite ourselves with them and in particular make alive that which continuously shall unite us with them? What does this mean? In other words, what does it mean when we now in our day consciousness call up wakefully what unites us with the dead."

In order to describe this, Rudolf Steiner himself says he has to use images and analogies to make himself even somewhat understood. He continues with the analogy: "What is it when we here in the physical sense world find what in itself does not belong to the continuing natural processes, but which we cannot possibly miss; that is, when we make ourselves images

---

1. See above (The Mystery of Death).

of what exists in nature, be it in artistic pictures, pictures of art, be it pictures as they in more recent times have been made by the camera, photographs. By making such images of the physical, sense-world, of beings who belong to the world, we add something to the processes of nature. Imagine how life is enriched by the fact that we make ourselves images of what otherwise is only a natural process. We long for these images; we long, apart from the natural processes, to have art in our world. We want to have an image of everything that we experience. Certainly the course of the world could continue also without them, but we *require* in a certain sense to make images of this world."

And now comes this extraordinary thought that if you take this analogy and transpose it to the relationship to the dead, we find that it is the images that we have, the images we make for ourselves of the dead, on which the dead depend. They cannot "live" without these images. Without them they would look to the earth and it would appear to them as void as the surface of the moon, empty, totally without anything alive to behold. But when these images are radiated toward them it is for them, in the words of Rudolf Steiner, "like the cathedrals, the works of art, which we in our ordinary life require in order not to be starved by being only part of the natural process"[1]. Our images are the cathedrals, the works of art, by which the dead can see the earth.

To my mind this is a truly shattering description. It may perhaps give us even more strongly the feeling that we cannot carry on as hitherto, but that we have

1. See above, Stuttgart, Nov. 22, 1915.

to practice image-making. Not only when we are art-
ists, nor when we are trying to relate ourselves to the
dead, but we have to learn image-making as a deliberate activity of our souls instead of having pictures
made in and for us constantly by the world. The development of electronics, in particular television, is
an attempt to stultify and paralyze our inner possibilities to make pictures actively. By the flick of a switch
the pictures are now made for us, are spewed into us,
covering up our own possibilities to develop them.

All this leads us further. We can live for a little
while with this concept of radiating our images to the
dead. If we then try to turn towards death, in as much
as we ourselves will experience it, we may do so at the
hand of Rudolf Steiner's very exact, precise descriptions. One can say that these descriptions are a fundamental plan for the spiritual exploration of the world
of the stars. In them lies a true inter-stellar program.

The moment of death has occurred; it is the moment that we look back upon for the long time that
intervenes after death as the greatest and the most
glorious moment of reality, the 'sunpoint' of our existence after life. When we have passed through various stages we come to the moment, the descriptions
of which are well known, when the experiences of the
so-called Kamaloca begin. I would like to remind us
of one small aspect of this in relationship to our
theme. This entrance is similar, and closely related to,
certain experiences of childhood. The growing child,
with his own developing body-schemata, begins to experience nature, discover nature, with its many plants
and begins to distinguish them, and also animals and
crystals. In a totally different way we enter the landscape, not of nature, but of the effects of our deeds on

other people. What our images have done to other people begins to shape itself like an enormous landscape around us. Fields of how deeply we reflected ourselves in others begin to spread out before us. Forests of kindness withheld or given begin to grow. Rivers and torrents of words in their effect upon others begin to curve within this landscape and gradually we begin to discover beings, spiritual beings; the dead with whom we were connected before we died ourselves. And now, *how* do we experience them? Rudolf Steiner says: "The dead ones" (with whom we were connected) "in this landscape now come towards us in their reality, but in order to recognize them we have to beam towards them the image we have had of them"[1]. Realities will meet us of those with whom we are connected, but we, so to speak, shall only know their face when we can radiate toward them the image which we have of them.

Yet another thing happens when this occurs. Out of this meeting in this landscape and out of the ability or inability to radiate the image to the realities we meet, something is born in our will. Something begins to take over which is now the *reality* of ourself: our ego. Our ego is now called upon to find the balance to this landscape and to what we have done to the people we knew. The will of our ego, which becomes unconscious when we are born again is now preparing an after-image of what we experience. This after-image is so molded and formed that it becomes in our next life what we will call our 'I'. We begin at this moment to form the image in which we will have to walk in our next existence. We are the creators of our own image.

---

1. See above.

Every such image of our ego is only an after-image trying to balance what we have experienced before. This balance is in the direction of a totality, so that in the end, the final image may comprise the totality of the ego. When it is said that man is created in the image of God, we speak of the intention that lies in the creation of every image which we make for ourselves so that we may fulfill it in our lives, that it may one day comprise the totality. Whatever our burden may be, however small, confined or restricted each one of these images has to be—tall or small, gifted or retarded, maimed or skillful—the vast varieties conceivable in these images are all contained and all needed. Each one of these has been molded by a creator together with the spiritual beings. Each one sets the conditions for an incarnation upon the earth. Who is this creator, whom we cannot know and yet call our 'I'? How can we relate ourselves to something that is working in us as a longing, as a guide or light, but unknown and invisible in its totality? How can we relate ourselves to this real 'I', which we can feel working and can acknowledge being the signatory of our personality?

Steiner's lecture from the 2nd of September, 1923 in London, called "Man as a Picture of the Living Spirit"[1] contains what I called the inter-stellar program for the human soul in most concise terms. There he describes the possibility of the most exact relationships which we can develop to this problem.

We are made aware—as indeed we could be in our ordinary life—of the fact that the guide is our 'little death'—is sleep. Sleep is one of the great riddles of human existence. It was in 1965 that Dr. König—

---

1. "Man as a Picture of the Living Spirit"—3 Lectures, London.

in the frame of a youth conference—was asked by many people what they could do to make more real what they *wanted* to do but always failed to do: how could they relate in deed and effort to all the wonderful exercises by Rudolf Steiner and so on? What could they really do so that they could handle them? Dr. König answered: "You must learn to go to sleep." If we could only make it possible to learn at least once per week to go consciously to sleep, deliberately, prepared, something that is done with full awareness,—many, I believe, could be helped toward the reality of their inner life and yet be part of the technological thinking which they, of course, must also practice. They would have to learn to go to sleep!

In the lecture just mentioned you will see that what we call ego is actually present in these dark places of sleep, in these intervening periods, already so important in childhood, but *not* our non-existence of the busy day, our work and life with which we usually identify ourselves. These moments of sleep, as we look back on them, must become like a canvas. The material on which to paint and practice our deliberate forming of images, which become meditative images, are painted on this darkness. After we are able to place this darkness before us appropriately, we begin to select the parts of our meditative image. These parts may of course vary. We may, for example, begin to remember how the plant has grown, how it has begun to develop the wooden part of its stem. We may then take from this process of plant growth the black wood of the stem. We will recollect this growing and dying activity; it will help us to place the part of the black wood before us as we have taken it away and separated it out. Through our activity we have gradually transformed it to something no longer belonging to the natural process. We have transformed it into part of our meditative image. Now to it we will perhaps add the roses. Slowly, on a totally different level through our deliberate activity, the three steps which deep in our consciousness our ego performs in our everyday memory begin to take place. When these "ingredients" for our image are added up, we exercise and practice spirit remembrance. As we place them together we practice spirit recollection. And when we can hold them against the canvas of the darkness of sleep where our ego is at work we practice spirit beholding. If we can hold to this meditative image throughout these three steps, painted as they are in a new light that is not borrowed from the day, we can use the strength to wipe the image away, to blot it out, to clean, to refurbish the canvas in the darkness in which our ego rests. For this process we may hear again the words which Rudolf Steiner related to it:

> I gaze into darkness.
> In it arises light.
> Living light.
> Who is this light in the darkness?
> It is myself in my reality.
> This reality of my Ego
> does not enter into my earth existence.
> I am only an image of it.
> But I shall find it again
> when I—with good will for the spirit
> shall have passed through the portal of death[1].

---

1. London, Sept. 2, 1923, "Man as a Picture of the Living Spirit."

We may say this image-making is not possible unless that which moves our inner hand and foot towards it is infused with a drop of our own death.
When we have wiped away with this drop of death the
picture we have at first assembled, then this canvas
will now mirror back to us—like the moon mirrors
the sun and the influences of the universe—something of that divine light that may warm our hearts,
that enlightens our heads,—that good may become
what we have to do here on earth. Our ego is of this
divine light. And then image begins for the first time
to show the power of its relationship to reality.

World Hunger—World Nourishment

1st of Advent, 1974, Beaver Run, PA

Good evening dear friends,

I want to speak about world hunger and world nourishment. Tonight is the first Advent Sunday of this year 1974 and at the same time it is the evening following the Camphill Community Day, which falls on the 30th of November. As so often, I had to ask myself: What can the purpose be of a spiritually striving community in our time? What can the purpose of *Camphill* be? Our community, despite the fact that through its work it is so closely related to everyday needs, is also in its spiritual pursuits seemingly often concerned with matters far removed from everyday concerns, and even removed from the needs which arise through our work.

This year one must also ask: *What* is it that we celebrate with Advent? There are not so many people in the world who celebrate Advent. Most people don't even know what it is. One can ask what do we *really* celebrate amidst these oncoming clouds of winter

31

darkness? Advent means the coming of something, and it no longer means the somewhat habitual expectation of a soothing experience of Christmas. It can no longer be merely an amelioration of our awareness that, in our true humanity, we are shut out of house and stable. Once again, we are where the community destiny of Camphill links with the message of Advent.

This year, perhaps more than in any previous year, the thoughts of many of us turned toward the appalling descriptions concerning world hunger. The answer of the world to the descriptions of the catastrophes of hunger was something of a mockery. We read about the Congress in Rome, where eleven hundred people, supposedly the cleverest and most influential heads of our so-called civilized world, (which will be regarded by history as one of the most barbarian that ever existed at any time) pretended to discuss the hunger of the world! The volumes of ineffectual stupidity brought forth at this occasion should be immortalized in the memory of men. But I am not going to dwell on this because the anger, dear friends, about what purports to be the leadership of our civilization is too great to really be able to put into words what one may feel about it.

I want to speak from a different angle. I would like to lift out some of the facts that were touched upon at this Congress; facts of the complexity with which the situation presents us. There are many other factors, equally complex, startling and puzzling and also equally offensive. I will only pick out two. The one concerns a deeply significant fact about our drinking water. It concerns the very small peninsula, reaching into the beautiful Lake of Constance, in

Germany, called the Reichenau. It has been one of the most fertile regions of the whole world and one of the most carefully and yet intensively cultivated areas. Probably even before there were historic records this area was cultivated. An aura of sanctity bestowed by this work lies around this region even today, and in many other regions around this area; places where the diligent, patient and devoted work of men have related for centuries to the gifts of nature. The Reichenau is a place of deep, black humus, at places about six feet deep. It has been referred to as one of the spaces of paradise upon earth since as early as the sixth, beginning of the seventh century when the great Irish bearers of Christianity came from Ireland to Europe to bring the understanding of Christianity to a Europe which at that time knew nothing of it. Columbanus and his twelve companions, amongst whom was St. Gall, St. Gallus, moved through this area. The Legend of Reichenau was as of a place of paradise that brings forth abundance through the cultivating activities of these early settlers. Ever since, the Reichenau has been one of the great horticultural places of the world. It was possible without exhausting its immense capacity for growth to reap harvests by well arranged rotations, sometimes three times a year, to bring forth vegetables in great abundance, which for a long time fed the people of the south of Germany, as well as many parts of Switzerland. Even today this continues to be done. The people there are almost always able to have at least two, even three, harvests for certain crops, every year. Most careful work is being done. But they can only do it, surrounded by the Lake of Constance—one of the largest lakes in Europe, by importing *all* the water which they need for drinking! Even though the Reichenau was abundant with fresh water to water their plants, the pure water of this island, on which this growth of plants is totally dependent, is gone, has become unusable for drinking, by the infiltration and total mineralization of the waters through artificial fertilization. The growth of these plants which today are being reaped often in larger amounts than hitherto is only possible, *has* only been possible over the last few decades, by the increasing number of artificial fertilizers which have gradually filtered through the ground and completely contaminated the water sources. The water is by now totally undrinkable for the population.

The second example which I want to mention is the increasing complexity of what was thought to be one of the greatest blessings to mankind, discovered and developed in the last decade, and came into widespread use in the last five or six years. These are the "wonder grains." These highly developed, hybridized grains are the result of years of study and work, most intensive and honest study by a host of scientists and in particular one man. It was hoped to be the answer to the hunger of the world, through an enormously increased yield, particularly of rice but also of bread grains. Wonder grains are only capable of this yield if supplied with enormous amounts of artificial fertilizers. Their potential yield was tested over two or three years, particularly in countries that so far never had any yields approaching these wonder-grain yields, in the East. Such grains were grown under exacting instructions by the agricultural experts who had produced them. Certain difficulties in following these instructions arose last year. The difficulties are due chiefly to the fact that the fertilizers needed for their growth are based on petroleum. Because of the rising price of oil it was impossible for these countries to buy the petroleum products and the fertilizers dependent on petroleum. The result was that the wonder grains, which nevertheless had been sown, yielded considerably *less* than the grains which had hitherto been planted, of the old types of grains to which the people had been accustomed. In addition, when in desperation long-term plans were made with the help of Western experts, plans which would economize the quantities needed, it was found out that in reality, despite or because of the enormous yield of these grains, the energy required to produce the necessary fertilizers exceeded (at least statistically) the energy which these grains could produce in human beings by giving them food. So, at the hand of only two such things the complexity and Babylonian confusion that exists surrounding this problem becomes very obvious.

When reading these heartbreaking things, when we hear and see them, we may ask how is it possible that it has come to this? How is it possible that one can't find answers? Perhaps we want to go even deeper, and ask: *What* feeds us? What is it that feeds us and the world? Are we all lying when at table we use the grace by Angelus Silesius: "The bread is not our food?"

But we must not forget that it continues and says: "What *feeds* us in the bread, is God's eternal Word, His Spirit and His *Life*"[1]. What feeds us is

_____

1. Angelus Silesius, 1624-77—German mystic and poet ("Cherubic Wanderer").

God's eternal Word! We know that, provided our being is open to the word of God, we can be fed by a morsel. There are very well known and well documented stories of people with a saintly disposition. When I was younger there was a simple peasant girl on the border of Austria called Therese of Konnersreuth. She was quite a simple girl who spent the last ten or fifteen years of her life in bed in total devotion, solely fed by the Holy Host which she received twice a week. This happened in our time. There are other people known to have lived on a handful of sustenance and not remained in bed. Somehow, that sustenance must have been sufficiently capable of carrying the forces of God, or of the Word, or of the Spirit, so that this was possible.

The question remains and I think we are justified to ask it on such a day as this: *What feeds us?*

Eating is a strange thing if we come to think of it. In the animal kingdom, particularly in the higher mammal, it is an extraordinary picture when, for instance, one of the large cats, a lion, or leopard, jumps upon its prey, tearing it down, feeding on it. It looks like an uncanny embrace, albeit a mortal one, with which this being takes its prey unto itself, burying its head into its victim's very entrails. It is an overwhelming gesture of destructive sympathy—to become *one* with the other thing! And we can sometimes feel that we too, though in a much more refined way—become one with a certain, small part of the world. It is, therefore, offensive if people eat in an ugly and greedy way because it is not appropriate to man to have this kind of obvious uniting of his inner juices with the substance of the world. Yet it is all "human." The moment we take the world into us we destroy it. It is dissolved, broken down. It becomes different. Part of it becomes part of us.

Indeed, we have three ways to unite with the world: when eating, breathing and in our sense-impressions. We unite with the world in these three forms; at the same time it is the way through which the dragon in us feeds. What is called—for want of a different association, the Dragon, the adversary of the being of Michael, lives supersensibly, invisibly in us, making use of our human organization in nutrition, in breathing and in the senses. He feeds on everything we as human beings do when uniting with the world. Everything that is, in which our own consciousness is not playing an appropriate part!

We could describe *how* the substances feed us with which we unite. Inhaling works on our senses. Nutrition dissolves; it ascends to the middle part of the brain from which our senses again receive some of their stimulus. In our middle system other parts of the nutritional substances, particularly the carbohydrates, are at work, and so forth. I do not want to go into the details, although these details belong to the most fascinating one can study. I am merely trying to point out, that we as human beings actually are meant all the time to be concerned with the spiritual aspect of our senses, our breathing and our nutrition. Then we shall begin to appreciate that hunger is not only the absence of food, it is also the *inability* to be nourished.

Of course we know that there have always been imbalances in the world and that there was often hunger and famine. These have been described in all phases of history, from the oldest to the newest times. The concept of the seven lean and seven fat years from the Old Testament is still shining into our times; a remarkable presence with which one counted and for which one made allowance. We have descriptions of the most terrible famines of all kinds and also of the undernourishment of children, right into the 19th century, in many parts of the civilized world. Yet I venture to say that no famine is the same. It is one of the continued superficialities with which we walk in the world, to believe that because people *were* hungry a thousand years ago, it is the *same* when they are hungry today. Famines are beings, just as other disasters are beings of a particular kind. And although famine and hunger always belong to an imbalance within the body of mankind and its relationship to its spiritual origin, the *way* in which this imbalance occurs at certain moments is different, is due to a different type of order, of justice, of retribution, of revenge, is due to different beings in the course of time.

I read quite recently the following account of a famine. It is quoted by one of our great contemporaries who died last year, Carl J. Burckhardt, in one of his books called *"Figures and Powers"*[1]. One of his essays is on the great humanist Willibald Pirkheimer, a contemporary of Luther, of Erasmus of Rotterdam, but also of Michelangelo and Leonardo. This was a tremendously interesting and important person, this Willibald Pirkheimer. Pirkheimer describes how he participated in one of the wars of the time, the so-called Swabian War at the beginning of the 16th century, when he was leader of a large troop of soldiers.

---

1. German—*Bildnisse*, S. Fischer Verlag, 1959. Burckhardt, born in Switzerland, 1891-1973, was a well-known historian, Diplomat and poet.

When they came to the Engadine, in Switzerland, one of the most beautiful regions of the earth, lush and rich, he saw two old women, survivors of the war, driving each morning a herd of starving children on all fours—because they were too weak to walk—upon the meadows, to have them graze what grass there was. Two old women, toothless survivors, driving a herd of children to the pasture! This is not the same famine of which we speak now. Of course, famines can be caused by floods, drought, war destruction. They were likened in the Middle Ages and thereafter, together with their accompanying disasters, the plagues and pestilences, to "the scourge of God." Well, as you know, in our time God has been declared dead, void and if there are famines, therefore, it can only be due to the mismanagement of man!

But they are there. And my question is: what can we do about them? As you know the answer of man today is, where there is a problem, have a congress where the experts come together. That is what happened in Rome. And then they appoint organizing groups and counseling services in which their wisdom is distributed at a charge to those who don't have it. Puzzled by the diversity, of course, which they then meet, they begin to counsel (not necessarily themselves, but those to whom they are sent) to exercise moderation, self-rationing and many other such aids.

A worthy effort is being made by an organization called "Oxfam." This is a conglomerate word consisting of "Oxford" from where it arises, in England, with "fam"—famine. It is student-carried and invites the students of the world to forego once a week their meal and to send the relevant savings to a central fund. There are many such things. One of the most interesting archbishops of the Catholic church in this country has tried, or is trying, to make the vast congregations in the Mid-West fast twice a week and use the savings to alleviate hunger. Of course, the difficulty is always where to send the money and how it will be distributed. It is then sent to some of the countries who need it most. One hears, for instance, that the accumulated funds that were sent to Ethiopia are now being used by the new military Junta that has shot the 60 advisors of the late emperor Haile Selassie and they have now bought some arms with some of the funds instead. That will happen many times if one saves in this form and whether it comes from Oxford or the Mid-West makes little difference. At any rate all these attempts can be summed up in one worthy but very puzzling attitude, and that is: they all relate to a redistribution of wealth. They all relate to a different kind of sharing of what there is, to a greater—more equitable—use of material resources, although no one knows quite how to do it. The thrust of it has to be voluntary, and if it is not to be voluntary, if it is to be through instituted rationing, you come into all kinds of insuperable, dangerous difficulties.

I could not help feeling, particularly last night, at hand of our bible reading[1], how this is related to the parable of the ten virgins. There you have, almost ironically, five with oil and five without oil. And then it turned out that five were somewhat foolish and when they ask: share with me, our lamps are empty, they are told: No, we can't give it to you, otherwise our lamps will be empty. How will you share in this

---

1. Matthew 25:1-13.

world? The moral of this parable is quite different. It is in the last line. The wise and the foolish virgins, both have one thing in common. They are dozing off when the bridegroom is late. At the end of the parable it quite clearly says: "Therefore, as you will never know the day nor the hour when He comes, be awake!" This mysterious advice in this parable says: "Be awake!"

It comes with the force of a cannon ball: *Be Awake!* One seems to know that this sound comes from the upper spheres of heaven, and what we understand of it is nothing but the poorest interpretation in our everyday mind. Perhaps, it might not be impossible to think that this call "Be Awake!" relates to the mysteries of hunger and world nourishment. I found the following description by Rudolf Steiner in one of his lectures to the workmen of the Goetheanum. Time and again these workmen were interested in nourishment, in food. Also on this day when he came in and said: "Now, gentlemen, what is your interest today?"—the question was, whether there is a relationship of nourishment through potatoes in different countries to nourishment in other European countries. Then Rudolf Steiner gave a series of fascinating lectures, because he himself did not want to stop after the first lecture, so he carried on with a second and third. The first comes under the general heading (in answer to this question): "The effect of protein, fats, carbohydrates and salts, the eating of potatoes, materialism and the hydrocephalus"[1]. Fairly early in this lecture, in relationship to a

---

1. "Cosmic Working in Earth and Man," R. Steiner, 6 Lectures to the Workmen. R. Steiner Publishing Co., London, 1952.

description of the working of fats and carbohydrates, Rudolf Steiner uses the following words: "What happens to the human being who either must go hungry or whose digestion is such that instead of the fats being deposited, they pass out of the body in faeces? A person who has not enough physical matter in his body becomes ever more spiritual. However, to become spiritual in this manner is not possible to be endured by the human being, for under these conditions the spirit consumes him, burns him up. He not only becomes thinner and thinner, but gases form in his organism and this condition leads eventually to actual delusions. And then the condition arises which is present in every hunger, "hunger madness." It always is a destruction by the Spirit, when man is ill in this way"[1].

I could feel that into my bones, dear friends, when I read these words and I can also tell you *why* I felt it in my bones: because I had this picture next to me. (The picture reproduced at the conclusion of this lecture). If you look at this picture you may ask yourselves: Look at the spirit in the eyes of this child. It *is* spirit, but it is the spirit that burns us to death. All the time there is spirit in us when we eat, when we take in substance. All the time there is spirit which tries to be present in every particle of the world that it has created. Spirit is and must be at work in our digestion. Spirit works or does not work in the way we take in proteins or carbohydrates, fats and salts. We order the spirit in us according to substances, however small or however large the portion that we

---

1. "Questions of Nutrition," September 22, 1923, Dornach. R. Steiner Publishing Co., London, 1952.

are enabled to eat. Either our body can be attuned to the spirit or be destroyed by the spirit. There is an immensely complicated process taking place in us in this nourishment and it is worthwhile to study it.

I want to read you one more word of Rudolf Steiner's. On a different day, in a different context, on July 18, 1923, he gave a lecture that bears two titles. The first title is: "How to Attain Knowledge of the Spiritual World" the second title is: "Questions of Nutrition, Potatoes and Root-Vegetables"[1]. *That* is one way to attain knowledge of the spiritual world! At the end of the lecture Rudolf Steiner says: "We actually do not build ourselves up out of the stuff of the earth at all; what we eat, we eat only so that we have a stimulus. In reality we build ourselves out of that which is above us. So that everything which the human being usually imagines comes *into* us as nourishment and which goes out again as nourishment, after it has nourished us, in the meantime it is working in us—that is not at all true. What we take into us is only a stimulus, a push, and we provide a kind of "counter push" below us and we build ourselves up, our whole body, out of the ether. All that we have in us is not filled out with the stuff of the earth. But it is so, that if something irregular occurs in this respect, if we take into ourselves too much nourishment, then the nourishment remains too long in us. Then we collect in us unjustified matter. We become corpulent, fat. If we take too little we have too little spirit and we therefore take too little of what we need out

---

1. "How do we gain specific knowledge of the spiritual world?" 4 Lectures to the Workmen; typescript edition only. July 18, 1923—On Nutrition, Questions about Potatoes and Beets.

of the spiritual world, out of the etheric world, through which we must build ourselves up."

This is so important to understand: We do *not* build ourselves up out of the substances of the earth and its matter, but we build ourselves up through that which is outside us in the ether. If we can follow this, the spirit is at work in us. In our bread there works the word of God and His life, and the Spirit *is* at work in hunger, and Spirit *is* at work in nourishment.

We can therefore really ask—and again I must point to this picture—what looks out of these eyes? Is it hunger or is it Spirit? And one might say, how does Spirit work in us as hunger and thirst? Would it perhaps be wiser to say: If something does *not* burn in us *like* hunger and thirst it is not Spirit, but something else, anything else. Spirit in us is of that same quality as is hunger and if it is not Spirit we could just as well leave it and do something else to entertain ourselves.

Let us recall something else. Rudolf Steiner was exact with every word. He did not speak, but *wrote* the first of his "Leading Thoughts" after the Christmas Foundation meeting, on the 17th of February 1924, the first of the Leading Thoughts with which it should be possible to prepare oneself inwardly for spiritual understanding. I am reading the first paragraph of this first Leading Thought; "Anthroposophy is a path of knowledge to guide the spiritual in the human being to the spiritual in the universe. It arises in man as a longing of the heart, of the life of feeling; and it can only be justified inasmuch as it can satisfy this inner need. He alone can acknowledge Anthroposophy, who finds in it what he himself in his own inner life feels compelled to seek.

Therefore, only those can be anthroposophists who feel certain questions about the being of man and of the world, as an elemental need of life, just as one feels hunger and thirst"[1].

I honestly believe that the world hunger of our time is directly the work of the Spirit and the abuse of the Spirit. It is burning in countless souls, millions of souls, in ways it should not do; namely, as bodily hunger, because we who should be aware of it are too saturated and full of nourishment. It is also because we are lame and crooked in our breathing, which is constantly influenced by our a-rhythmic kind of life, our over use of cars, the irregular erratic way in which we live and move, including sports! And we are paralyzed by the gluttony of our senses which constantly want to enjoy themselves. I believe that world hunger is *caused* by the rejection of the Spirit, which now seeks, because it cannot find *conscious* placement in mankind, disastrous and destructive other forms in the body of mankind. Perhaps world nourishment would suffice if the Spirit would be diligently cared for in the same way as we care for our bodies, for our jobs and for our seemingly overriding duties. If we would spend a tenth of the time on serving the Spirit as we use to tend and serve everything else, perhaps it would induce a sufficient number of other people to hear the word: "Be Awake!"

Perhaps only in an awakening community spirit may we find some means to lessen the world hunger

---

1. Anthroposophical Leading Thoughts: Anthroposophy as a Path of Knowledge: The Michael Mystery. R. Steiner Publications Co., London. Translation: George and Mary Adams.

which otherwise will destroy not only this child in Ethiopia but also the child in all of us. There will then be no Christmas and one will never know why we should celebrate Advent.

Thank you very much. Please look at the picture.

Hungry Ethiopian Child

Michael in Our Time

September 29, 1974, Beaver Run, PA

Dear friends,

I would like to begin with the image of Michael and the dragon. It is an image familiar to many people; it has often been painted, sculpted, described; in the course of time it has tended to become evermore earthly. In a certain sense it is to be found as St. George's fight with the dragon—and St. George really depicts the patron saint of England. These images point obviously to a great spiritual fact, a fact which does not only take place once as if one fight had occurred, but as a continuing event. It is a fight to restore the purposes of the original intentions of creation. One may, out of one's own experience, out of the very picture, but also through human life, have a glimpse, a feeling that it is indeed an image of a tremendous spiritual fact, an ongoing fact. Historically it has become a picture. This picture lived as part of the environment, more so in Europe and the east of Europe than here. Even as a picture it was alive—it

47

conveyed strength and moral impetus to many people in Europe, until about the 18th century. Gradually it became nothing but the echo of a legend, a pale concept of what this image should represent. It became a kind of superstitious thought—something that finally one could no longer link to the realities of life. But while this continued to be so for most people, a subtle change began to take place.

This change started to seep into the spiritual life of man and his cultural endeavors at the end of the 19th century. There had been a complete dearth of reality of this image for about 100 years, except for weak traditions and legends. But since the end of the 19th century something began again to answer if one turned to images of Michael, chiefly to his fight with the dragon or to look to Michael holding the scales. It seems as if new life would well forth again from the source over which stands the word: "Michael." This is only a feeling—a slight kind of response. But it is the beginning, one may assume, of a new development, of a new way of relationship to the being, to the meaning, to the power, of Michael.

It is from Rudolf Steiner, that we have more or less learned to use the name of Michael again. Even for us, this is still uncertain and yet in a majestic way it promises something. Perhaps the most important first new experience of the powers of Michael as a supersensible spiritual force occurs *within* the sphere of our senses.

Let us imagine the strange situation we have to face as those who are interested in the spirit: that one is confronted with a seeming duality which we can in totally inappropriate ways make into a kind of dogma by the misuse of concepts. This can happen when we speak about the physical world and the spiritual world; the world of the senses and the *super*sensible.

Let me say a word about the dragon. We recently had occasion to suggest amongst ourselves that we should again look at four important lectures Rudolf Steiner gave in Vienna, at Michaelmas 1923, called "Anthroposophy and the Human Gemut"[1]. You may be astonished that there is an English title with a German word in it, but I think all anthroposophists on the German and English side concerned with translations have tried their hardest to find an equivalent of the German word 'Gemut' in English and have not been able to come up with anything useful. 'Gemut' means an area within the human soul that is related to and permeated by feeling, but is not in itself feeling, but rather a mode of existence in which the life of the heart is the main informer of all that goes on. It is about this Rudolf Steiner speaks, and these four lectures are fundamentally related to Michael and his fight with the dragon. I will quote a few things from these lectures tonight.

I would like to describe what Rudolf Steiner tells us about the dragon. We have to imagine the dragon to be a name, a designation, for spiritual beings who, a long, long time ago in evolution undertook to emancipate their own will from the will of the God-head. In doing so they became contrary to the plan of creation. Not because they did so, but because they did it too early, before the appointed time. They attempted to bestow this ability in varying degrees upon mankind. However, these beings then could no

---

1. Title of latest edition: "*Michael and the Soul-Forces of Man*"—Vienna, Sept. 27, 28, 30, October 1, 1923.

longer live in the same way in the spiritual world and in those kinds of spiritual forms appropriate to the spiritual world from which they had wanted to separate. In the first fight which the being of Michael had with them, he threw them out of this untenable situation, from this sphere in which they were and the great difficulty and embarrassment was: Where should they go? Now the difficulty was: They did not fit anymore—there was no suitable form in which they could dwell in that place whence they had emancipated themselves. But there was no form available elsewhere in which they could be. And so, as a kind of compromise, these beings were thrown into earthly existence. The earth was quite different then, but it was there. Earth existence was also not meant for them. It did not really provide forms which they could use to live in, at least not fully. The design of the earth, the becoming physical of the earth, assuming physical forms and becoming increasingly visible and tangible to the senses, could not possibly fit those spiritual beings who had been transferred there. So they could only live invisibly amongst the elements of the visible world. Thus they began to inhabit forms which were only developed to a certain degree and which today are quite unthinkable and cannot be conceived here upon the earth, but at that time they were possible: somewhat snake and alligator-like, amphibian-like and bird-like, a kind of a mixture but these forms never became definite or capable of accepting living beings, never developed to the point of living within physical density. These fallen beings, however, remained within these forms, invisibly, up to this day. They still are invisibly present in these forms, everywhere in nature. But they did not belong to the earth, they did not really belong to nature, and they had of course a tremendous task to fulfill in order to get on with their own self-proscribed purpose. They had to try to evolve, to be partakers of evolution. But they could not do that by themselves, because they had no direct possibility to participate in those evolving forms whose intention was to become visible, physically visible and tangible. They could not do anything with these. Neither could they do anything directly with man.

But they could do one thing. I am describing (still using Rudolf Steiner's explanation) the picture which in ever weaker images one could have until the 18th century. The fallen beings could do one thing. Man takes, *has* to take, nature into himself in three ways. We all have three ways to relate to nature. One, via nutrition, by taking natural substances into ourselves and making them our own. Two, by inhaling the natural environment of the air, which we have made so unnatural by now. And, three, through our senses we also take in nature. But the dragon can enter into our own existence through what we take into ourselves in these three ways.

This dragon-like process continues in us as the result of how we assimilate the natural processes through nutrition, through breathing and through our senses. Thus, the dragon has become a participant in and a developer of these processes in us. He is supersensibly in us as a kind of continuer of the nature processes; sitting somewhere in them as a constant developer of his purposes. One experienced it like this roughly until the 18th century. At the same time one was permeated by the conviction that all this which had been created as visible nature through the millennia was not the real or full being of nature. The *real* being of man, as the crown of creation, was felt to be divine and therefore his divinely created "upper" part would be in constant Michaelic combat with his "lower" part, the part of the dragon existence within him.

The verse of the Calendar of the Soul for this week begins with the words: "Nature, your motherly being I carry it within my will's existence"—"Natur, dein mutterliches Sein, ich trage es in meinem Willenswesen." These words already mean the beginning of a quite new era. For during the last century yet another fight took place of the Archangelic host around the being of Michael with the forces of the dragon, a fight which has to take place ever and again. This last battle took place in the middle of the 19th century, lasting decades, so Rudolf Steiner tells us, beginning with the year 1841 and ending with the Autumn of 1879. A new phase of the relationship between the dragon forces in nature and in man began with this battle. A new era of Michaelic reality also began.

Rudolf Steiner speaks about this new era when he tries, as he so often does, to awaken in us by the use of his words what we have taken with us from the spiritual world. He uses the following words, describing the situation after the end of the 19th century, the time in which we live. "In man lives an etheric image of Michael which leads the actual fight in man, through which man can gradually become free in this Michael battle. Because it is not Michael who leads that battle but the human surrender to this image and the image of Michael which is created through this surrender"[1]. These are the powerful

_____

1. Lecture 1, 27th Sept. 1923—"*Michael and the Soul-Forces of Man*".

words Rudolf Steiner uses. Then he gives another description: "In the last third of the 19th century the Michael image became so strong in man that the matter of directing his feelings upward and rising to the Michael image came to depend on his goodwill, so to speak"[1]. Then he says a few paragraphs later what takes place within one if one tries this: "I concentrate my Gemut upon this glowing figure. I let its light stream into my Gemut, and thus my illumined and warmed Gemut will bear within it the strength of Michael. And out of a free resolution I shall be able, through my alliance with Michael, to conquer the dragon's might in my own lower nature." Rudolf Steiner goes further and says: "In doing that, one begins to be able to think in reality about this image, have thoughts, light thoughts about it." And a further step, (Rudolf Steiner's words again): "These radiant thoughts of Michael would then be the first pronouncers of man's entering again into the spiritual world"[2]. So, we can say, perhaps: I can, if I am willing.

But how do I will it? Obviously not by just saying: "I will." It is *good will* that is needed and of a special kind—a special effort is needed. My question is really this, on the basis of all we have heard: how does this special effort begin? How can we strive toward a supersensible encounter with Michael in the world of the senses? As always Rudolf Steiner is most explicit if we only read him carefully, if we are willing to let ourselves be guided by the train of thought that he offers. He tells us that our Gemut which obviously is the one thing into which this image must shine is only useful

---

1. Ibid.
2. Ibid.

in this situation if we can in some way deal with it so that it is taken hold of, if we can learn to manipulate our Gemut in such a way that it can be taken hold of. Let us try to picture to ourselves what usually happens with our Gemut and to our senses. Let us particularly turn to our sense-experiences. How do sense experiences usually work for us? We can stand under a beautiful sky, see the sunset, or a field waving with its ears of grain in the wind; we can see and enjoy the ripples of colors; we can stand under such an impression for a long time and with great enjoyment. But that does not mean that we may not be totally asleep with regard to what we are *meant* to see if we would only perceive and not merely stare. All such experiences, however sincerely surrendered to, when they enter into us via eye, ear, taste or any other senses, are food for the dragon. The dragon in us requires our sense experiences to nourish him. He avidly eats up what enters us through our coming into touch with nature, unless *we can accompany* our sense impressions differently.

All things that are man's environment need man. Everything that is created needs to pass through us. I would like to quote a poem by Rainer Maria Rilke in order to describe how this can be meant: "All must go *through* man." Rilke himself has written about the intentions of some of his poems. He has very clearly described what has just been pointed to. He knew nothing Rudolf Steiner had said by that time, he was by no means an anthroposophist and any talk of spirituality in the usual sense would have been deeply distasteful to him, as was any ordinary church belief. Yet he was a being wrestling with an almost shattering kind of honesty concerning his work (not necessarily concerning himself, but his work). You can read in his letters about his intentions and not only find it expressed in his poetry. His central work, perhaps, are the Duino Elegies. They have an amazing history and in the Ninth Elegy, from which I want to quote, Rilke says the following:

> "Earth, isn't this what you want: an invisible re-arising in us? Is it not your dream to be one day invisible? Earth! invisible! What is your urgent command, if not transformation? Earth, you beloved one, I will! Oh, believe me, you need your Springs no longer to win me: a single one, just one, is already more than my blood can endure. I've now been unspeakably yours for ages and ages. You were always right, and your holiest inspiration is Death, that friendly Death. Look, I am living. On what? Neither childhood nor future are growing less . . . . . Supernumerous existence wells up in my heart"[1].

Earth, invisible! Could it be that there is in the earth, in the being of nature, in all which has come about through eons, this constant call that we may transform it as it passes through us? Could it not be, that with the help of man everything created around him, can and should be lifted up to a higher existence, which it could not reach without him? Everything in nature asks that man so see and experience it that what is magically held imprisoned within it

---

1. Rilke, Duino Elegies—English translation F.B. Leishman and Stephen Spender, 1939 by W.W. Norton & Co., Inc.

would be released by the way he looks at it, would be freed, would re-arise within him. When this does not take place, the dragon feeds.

What does this mean? What here is the Michael-power? What does it mean, to be taken hold of in the Gemut by such sights and thoughts, as if by something physical? Let me read again a few lines of Rudolf Steiner's: "The Michael-powers can only be taken hold of when man makes himself, with his love-filled will, a tool for the divine spiritual powers. For the Michael-powers do not want man to pray to them. They want man to unite himself with them. This man can learn to do"[1].

How? Our reaffirmation, however often under-taken, our renewal of sense experiences for all this—must contain a consecutive process by which we can realize, step by step, an alignment with something that has recognizably been the origin of our effort but which we time and again seem to lose as we proceed. We must be able to oversee how we sense, how we employ, unfold and direct our senses.

We have often heard from Rudolf Steiner, repeated by Dr. König, that one of the necessary steps is that we must wonder about what we see! Wonder, awe, astonishment. Are we so often astonished by what we see? Is it possible that we could foster wonderment and astonishment? Is it possible, for instance, that we become aware of our sense-processes as a frightfully interesting development in our soul-lives instead of merely accepting them? Is it possible that we can learn to observe ourselves to such an extent that we also learn to understand that when we

---

1. Lecture 2, Sept. 28, 1923—"Michael and the Soul-Forces of Man."

look at a sunset, or at a wonderful field where the wind blows over the grain, we have looked at it with astonishment and wonder? Perhaps it would be possible if one would compose a song, if one has *not* used astonishment, to try to find a different kind of tuning in to the impression, to renew it, refresh it. Maybe we could honestly affirm: There was no astonishment; but when I use myself, my senses differently, like this, it could be with astonishment. But mostly we are *so* sure, so imbued with the certainty that we *know* how we shall experience with our senses; so we don't do it. We don't treat the senses *themselves* as a landscape of wonder, to be explored. We are so self-satisfied that the way we are using our senses always seems to be the right way. And while we are willing to experiment with little bits of minerals in a lab, with one of our holiest parts, our senses, we are usually not willing to test how they serve us. One neither can nor should do this all the time, of course. Rudolf Steiner thought that one should do it sometimes, as exercises. I do not need to tell you further about it, all of you can read it, many of you have.

And yet at Michaelmas, perhaps it is justified once again to return to these four great steps which should always evolve in our sense experiences: To walk into wonder so that with the help of wonder we begin to be aware of some kind of reverence taking hold of us and of our senses, a reverence that we have not even expected at first. We shall then experience something which tells us more than we see; that is no longer anymore something we merely see, something that happens to us merely in the sphere of the eye—but that *in* what we see we begin *to see something of the wisdom of what we see.* We certainly shall *see* it, not think it; but it is a higher, enhanced, light-thought-seeing process. And gradually we can live, at least for a moment, in the tangible acceptance of being one with what we see. We shall feel one with the course of the world. It cannot come by itself. We are prevented from experiencing it without effort. Rudolf Steiner calls it the cardinal sin of always doing everything too early, dragon-like.

It is the continued work of the Fall which causes us to be as we are and Michael wages continued battle against the dragon around and in us, until we ourselves can wage it. Always to want to do too early! Accepting too early! Being too early! The continuous process of not accepting that a good thing needs its time. A seed must pass through the times of its rhythms. Experience must wax through the stages of our being. We know this. But how can we learn to cooperate with it?

What was meant in the moment when Goethe told Schiller: "I am not thinking about the archetypal plant, I see it!" What was it, when Rilke stood day after day before a cage in which a panther walked up and down, up and down, until the walking and the gait so much entered into him that he could write in his poem—not about that panther—but about the *being* of the panther, caged by man. What is it that allows one to see not only what one sees but what allowed the thing one sees to appear? One begins to perceive within what one sees what *motivates* this thing. One does this not by psychological interpretation, but by seeing, deeply seeing, what is at work, what will is at work behind what there *is*, what I *see, hear* or *smell.*

We must learn to look at the world of the senses in such a way that we can see the will in everything there is. And by seeing the world of the weaving will in creation, we make the first step to look *through* the world of the senses into the supersensible. We can see with our eyes what the will is in each thing, and this is a supersensible experience. But for that it is necessary that we do not only enjoy our senses and remain there. I do not say we shall *not* enjoy it. I say we shall not *remain* at our enjoyment of the senses. We shall be informed by them and thereby enable ourselves to pass into a stage of wonder, which then opens into reverence. This allows us, for a moment, to see in a thing the will which is at work within it. We no longer see the lily as it grows in the field, not only the passing dog or the wolf, but that which makes the wolf, wolf-like—the dog—doglike, what moves within them as its will to be. When this sense experience reaches to the world of will around us—and if we then are taken hold of still further in our super-sense experience, as if a physical thing would take hold of us and lift our hand from here to here, so our senses must be taken hold of by the will—in that will we shall then hear, taste, touch the wisdom which has made this will to be as it is. The sense impression which has become a gateway to the supersensible is no longer what it was, is no longer a dead weight in the gulf of our senses. Rudolf Steiner describes this third stage: "To feel oneself in wisdom-filled unison with the world laws"[1].

One can have the impression that this is something that would perhaps be good to try, or is worthwhile, whatever it may be. But how? How does one apply it? How does one go about it? It can be very embarrassing if we try it out at certain moments. It would

---

1. Reference, Sept. 30, 1923, Lecture 3 (above).

not be good to look at each other and begin there! It is altogether a very sensitive thing to attempt any such thing with human beings. Yet imagine, particularly those friends who have worked with children and who have been to many College Meetings[1], that a certain amount of this process takes place when a College Meeting is taking place in all earnestness—one turns to a child and on the basis of the information from the case history one looks first at the physical make-up of this child. One "eats" it up, tastes it, smells it, until one can almost feel that one begins to move in the way the child moves. The will of such a child seems accessible to one; one moves in its being and in the wisdom that made it move.

But it is a very different thing to do that alone, or at random, or without, if I may call it so, the controlling presence of a community. Rudolf Steiner, who knew that it would have to be tried, that it would have to become accessible to many, many people, quite concretely described how we can all go about this at first and in what manner, in what hygienic, healing manner this process could take place. When he spoke about these matters they culminated in a cycle called "The World of the Senses and the World of the Spirit"[2]. At that time he prepared to deliver the Calendar of the Soul. These lectures from which I quoted before and from which I will quote again go hand in hand with the Calendar of the Soul. They complement each other. In the Calendar of the Soul Rudolf

---

1. The College Meeting is a specific "child study" meeting that has been developed as a pillar of Camphill life, especially in the schools, and has been written about by Dr. König in the Camphill Movement book and in other articles.
2. "The World of the Senses and the World of the Spirit"—6 lectures, Hannover, December 27-31, 1911, January 1, 1912.

Steiner turns the Michaelic attempt to live in self-stimulated, self-conscious awareness in the circle of one's senses toward the year of the soul.

Let us imagine the year of our individual existence; that means not the twelve months, but that "year" which spans one of our incarnations. This is the year of our individual being. That year is conditioned by many, many things which we do not know because we are it ourselves, but we can bring it into an alchemic relationship with the continuous mankind-embracing course of the year through the Calendar of the Soul. All indications by Rudolf Steiner concerning Michael in our time are closely related to the fact that this Michaelic power can and should be experienced in relationship to the course of the year and its festivals. If you and I want to celebrate a real Michael festival, we will only be able to do so when we do not speak anymore in images and quotations but when we will be able to think Michaelic thoughts; namely those thoughts which on the basis of wonder, reverence, and experience of the wisdom-filled world have made us able to reach to the will of creation.

Let me read this paragraph by Rudolf Steiner: "We can point to the fact that that which can lead to a Michaelmas festival must be an event of the Gemut, a happening of the Gemut which can experience the course of the year in reality. Do not say, however, as you place this thought before your soul, that you already experience it. Say it only when you have indeed taken anthroposophy into yourself in such a way that anthroposophy has taught you to look at each plant, at each stone, differently. Differently than you looked before at each plant and stone. Say it only, that you can celebrate a Michaelmas festival, after anthroposophy has taught you to look at all of human life in its becoming, differently, newly"[1].

This newness begins in the world of the senses. It can begin in the world of the senses in relation to living with the course of the year and the festivals. It can begin so that we become aware of the forces of growth and becoming, of decline and wasting in the world-will. Nowhere is this lifted up into our minds more grandiosely than through the course of the year. In living deeply into spring and summer, thence into the declining time of fall and winter, we live with this world-will on the widest possible scale. We must learn to do so more consciously.

In streaming out in summer we are stimulated to use all our senses to the fullest. At the same time we unite with the World-Word that is at work in nature. I think we can find in this world-fact the reason for Michael's fight with the dragon which pertains to our time. For this was not always so. It is quite new that this is so. The World-Word sounded from different directions to men than from nature. But thirty years after him who is the forerunner and countenance of the Christ, after Michael fought his last battle, thirty years after 1879 that event began to take place in the aura of the earth which is called the coming of the etheric Christ. It is to prepare ourselves for the experience of the World-Word that now appears in the ether-world, permeating the aura of the earth, that these Michael beings, this Michael strength is meant to enter into us. Why, dear friends, should we add to the festivals of the year, to Christmas, Easter, Whitsun, to St. John's time with the streaming out into the

---

1. Oct. 1, 1923, lecture 4—"Michael and the Soul-Forces of Man."

cosmos, why should we add to them in fall, the Michaelmas festival, if it were not to prepare ourselves for the Advent of our time, for the continuous coming of the Christ in the ether world? This coming now works in the earth which is His body. These are the elements even if we can only think them haltingly which we can take into ourselves, together with the constant attempt to re-enliven the images of Michael, with the never ending hope, that the time will not be too far away when real Michaelmas festivals can be celebrated.

Thank you.

LECTURE FOUR

Song of the Earth
An Advent Address

Camphill Village, December 9, 1973, Copake, NY

(dedicated to poet Felix Braun)
+ November 29, 1973

Felix Braun, Vienna, 1968

Dear friends:

I am not too sure whether the time of the year in which we are, Advent, and the time of the world in which we are, really requires anything new or surprising to be told. One feels that one should rather consolidate, firm up, if possible, what lies in our souls.

Today the weather with the rainstorm, relentless for most of the day, pressing from outside upon us, is like an illustration of a particular path that belongs to Advent. In a wonderful way one can experience the strength unleashed by nature. The wind in the trees, the rain, it is so different from what we experience in summer. Remember how it is on a really hot summer night when we are together here? After the long hot day we wear the thinnest of clothes and all the time the heat is working upon us from outside. We are sweating, it is as if all the time we would flow over, as if we would not have definite outlines to our body but as if we would be softened by this watery substance, by the sweat that tries to unite us with the world around. But today, every time one surrenders oneself to the storm one can experience how it tries to push one in, it tries to make one far more defined and determined than usual, so that one has to hold fast to oneself. One even tries to huddle together around the core of warmth, around the core which one feels is oneself. At such times one can feel lonely. One can discern, if one is awake and careful, that this loneliness, this being thrown back upon oneself, asks something. By being pressed together, thrust back upon oneself, one is asked to listen to something like a deeply known music.

There is a very justified reaction that comes with this type of coldness. One wants to overcome loneliness. One wants to overcome singleness. There arises the natural feeling: let's huddle together around some kind of light, around some kind of candle. Let us be together around a light. That is also very real for the experience of Advent: let us be together around a candle.

I knew a man of whom I want to tell you tonight. He was the most specific Advent-man I have known. I wish to dedicate this evening to him because he has just died. He died on the 29th of November, in a hospital in Austria called Klosterneuburg. He was 88 years of age. For many significant moments in many years of my earlier life we were great friends. He was a well-known poet in my country of birth, Austria, and his name was *Felix Braun*. Felix means the happy one; Felix Braun. He was considerably older than I and yet we had a very special relationship. If anything he was a little taller than I, only very thin. There was something brittle in the way he looked, one was always afraid that if he made too quick a movement he may just break somewhere. He had large, very talking hands with which he wrote his poetry with beautiful, careful, slow letters on white sheets of paper. I still have a number of these manuscripts. He had a very strange look, dear friends. And if I compare his looks to an animal, you must not laugh because it is not meant as a joke at all. When you looked at him in profile, he gave the deeply moving impression of a lamb. He looked like a lamb and he was a bit like a lamb. He was an infinitely tender person who couldn't do any harm to anybody or anything. In his beautiful autobiography which, typically, is called "The Light of the World"[1] (Das Licht der Welt), he describes two occasions when as a young person he lost his temper. Two occasions! And he deeply regretted it for the remainder of his life. He was an extremely erudite, learned person. He was a Doctor of Philosophy and was well acquainted, both in Austria as well as in Germany, with most of the famous poets and writers who were his contemporaries, some of whom I also was permitted to know. He often told me about his meetings and conversations with them. He wrote many books, books of poetry, four novels, several books of short stories and two big volumes of dramas, some of which were written in verse, quite a number of which were performed in the famous theaters in German-speaking countries in Europe.

I met him for the first time in the house of some friends in a suburb of Vienna when I was a student of art. We sometimes gathered in the evening in that house and listened to music, often newly composed by some of this circle of friends, or did some poetry reading. We had also great fun together and discussed and conversed about what interested us in the world, particularly in art. On one of these evenings we were told, with a certain amount of respect and awe, that he was coming. He did not "belong" to this circle, it was an honor that on that evening he was willing to read to us, and that we would be the first ones to hear his new play, which had been accepted to be performed in one of the theaters in Vienna. And so he came. We all went up into the garden behind the house, a steep garden planted up a hill around which there were vineyards, set among beautiful fruit trees and beds of flowers. At the end of the garden was a lit-

---

1. Felix Braun, November 4, 1885—November 29, 1973, Austria. "Das Licht der Welt"—Autobiography 1949, not published in English.

tle hut. In this hut could sit 15 people or thereabouts, many of us on the floor. It was a simple round wooden hut with only very thin walls on three sides, a summer hut where one could shelter from the sun or from a sudden rain. It was a warm evening, we went there to be away from any disturbance or noise and there he came with his manuscript. He had to bend down to get through the low door. He wore a dark, rather poor suit and greeted us all in a way that I would wish to convey to you as lovingly as I can. He greeted everybody, also those whom he already knew well, as if it would be the first or the last time. He greeted them by looking deeply into their eyes, shaking their hands several times and at the same time holding his head bent sidewards as if he wished to excuse himself from altogether occupying any place whatsoever. In his whole demeanor he tried to blot himself out and allow, instead of himself, the one he was just greeting to live fully in him. After he had greeted us all he sat down at a little table where a candle was lit, and in the candlelight, in the increasing dusk, he began to read his drama in verse, the title of which is also the name of an emperor: "Charles V"[1]. He read with immense expression, living totally in the words, given totally up to the scenes that occurred in these words and which in his beautiful, classic style rolled from his lips in an intonation of song rather than ordinary speech. This drama unfolded before us. When he read the role of the emperor, or the villain, the woman, or the hero, he *was* every one of these persons. And time and again he looked up from

1. Drama "Charles VII" 1936. No English publication. [Charles V, Emperor of Germany, King of Spain 1500-1558].

his manuscript, his head turned to the side, his big eyes looking upward, reciting the words rather than reading them from the manuscript, and so he held us spellbound for two or two and a half hours. This was the first time I met him.

I met him on many more occasions, sometimes in the house I have described to you, also on a few occasions alone. We had very intensive talks, particularly about poetry, and a kind of friendship began even though I was so much younger than he. Some kind of search that was common to us both created this friendship.

Then, as you know, Austria was completely absorbed into Germany by annexation through Hitler. I went away soon thereafter and had a very interesting, but also difficult time. There were already strong threads to friends who later on in Scotland began to build up Camphill as a community. But meanwhile I threaded my way through all the many complicated circumstances and difficulties, also dangers, through a number of countries and finally landed in England. There, having no money at all and only a few connections that could be helpful to me, I was offered what was then called a "hospitality" for refugees. This was in a tiny little place, a hamlet with a few houses in the Lake-district of England, which is a most wonderful area with beautiful lakes and wonderful hills and mountains and forests, a beautiful area in which many of the English poets of the past lived, like Wordsworth. There, in a tiny house that had stood empty for quite some time, I could live. It had a tiny bedroom and a tiny kitchen, and there I stayed. Some of the people who were organizing all this and felt responsible for my conduct until I found my own feet, came and visited me from time to time. On one of these visits one of these friendly ladies of the neighborhood, a real English lady, came to me and said: "Well, you will be glad to hear that in walking distance there is another Austrian refugee who has come here two weeks ago and if you care, you could probably get together as you are countrymen and could talk. He is a doctor and you will probably enjoy meeting him." Well, I went there and found that this other refugee was Felix Braun. He lived within walking distance of about 15 or 30 minutes, also in a tiny cottage, also enjoying "hospitality", and tried to work.

Can you imagine what it means for a poet and writer, to suddenly be placed away from his own language, from his very substance of expression and nobody around him understands him? So we met. We met for many months almost daily and our real friendship began, for I was almost his only audience. He would read his poems to me. He would tell me of his plans. We made long excursions and we discussed many things concerning his books. I sometimes gave him something to read that I had written and we tried to assess our writings and our situation and that of the world.

The first time that I had seen him, as I have told you, he was reading his play by the light of a candle in this beautiful little place in Vienna. When we met again he himself became a kind of candle to me, in the light of which I could walk in the region of poetry, of art, of thoughts. For it was also for me not an easy time to be in a new country and acquire a new language. It was as if all the time Advent was around one, so that even one's own language could not be understood, and it made one feel lonely.

After several months our ways parted again. Since then I have only seen him twice more, in Vienna, a few years ago. Although greatly honored by the City of Vienna and by various prizes received for his poetry, he was quiet lonely. He was living alone, waiting until his time would be fulfilled. I will not tell you the details of the talks we then had, some of which are deeply written into me. I wanted tonight to tell you about him and dedicate to his memory these Advent thoughts which I want to recall in us as something I believe, all of us know, deep down in ourselves.

Let me refer to Advent in general and ask, what *is* Advent, what does it mean? Advent means the coming of something. Advent means something important is coming. I believe we feel, when we experience the time in which we live something of this expectancy. Even the wind, the pressures from outside, seem to announce the feeling that we must be aware, in a position of expectancy, for the coming of something. We could say we expect Christmas to come. We expect the festival of the image of man as a child. In order to comply with our inner urge when thrust back on ourselves, we light candles, one for each Sunday. But we ought to try to light candles *in* ourselves every day. A candle for someone, a candle for something, a light every day. What is a candle? A candle is an object which can be bigger or smaller, wide or narrow, consisting of some substance which burns, of wax or some such substance. So that it can burn but not burn away in a flash we must put into the middle something that retards this burning; that is the wick. It is actually the wick which burns, slowly absorbing into itself the burnable substance. I want us to take it quite

exactly when I say, Advent intends us to light candles.
There is a substance that wants to light up and burn,
but would burn away in vain, unless we can place this
wick into the middle that slowly absorbs the burning
substance and thus burns away. There are two marvelous lines by Shakespeare: "There lives within the very
flame of love a kind of wick or snuff that will abate
it"[1]. There needs to be some kind of retarding element. This retarding element, set into the middle of
the burning substance, of love, makes it burn not
quite as much, holds us back, gives us the possibility
of light, of constant light, of light that can be rekin-
dled.

Remember, please, the gospel from Matthew,
Chapter 24, Verses 1-51. Remember how a World-Ad-
vent is apocalyptically described, that moment when
even the sun, the moon and the stars will no longer
shine because of the force of the wind, the force of
pressure from without, the force of alienation. It says
in the gospel: Let no one return even to his home.
Have pity on the women who are then bearing a child
or nourish babes, for it is the time when we indeed
must expect the coming of something, the advent of
something[2]. One can say, when reading this part of
the gospel: What then, amongst these apocalyptic
words, is there comparable to the candle? What is the
light in that gospel reading? We can *hear* this candle,
not only see it. It is like a song, it is like the music that
we can hear in our loneliness, even during the time of
our own, much more modest advent. The music that
we hear is the *real* folk song of mankind; it is one that

---

1. Hamlet, Act IV, Scene 7, Lines 1-15, 1-16.
2. Matthew 24, verses 17-20.

lives in every human soul and is expressed in words
that you know from the gospel readings. It should be
sung, for it is sung by every human heart if we only
hear it: "And they will see the Son of Man coming in
the clouds of heaven with great power and glory"[1].
That is the song of the earth, which every human being who is born can experience within as his own folk
song when he listens to the onrush of Advent in himself.

What does this wonderful folk song mean? It
speaks about the coming in the clouds. We begin in
the ether-clouds of our thoughts to *see* something. I
am not sure whether we can really call it thinking, but
it is a thinking activity that makes it possible, when the
pressure of Advent is upon us, that in the clouds of
our ordinary thoughts we begin to discern the ether-
clouds from which this folk song of the soul speaks
and rings. Then comes the seeing of the Son of Man,
and that is like the onrush of the warmth of our soul
when we, being pressed upon from the outside, begin
to realize our own warmth of soul. Then something
like the Son of Man can be seen with the eyes of our
soul. When it speaks about the power and the glory
we can feel in it the depth which this Son of Man bestows upon us, overriding wind and loneliness. Thinking is the light of the heights in the ether-clouds;
feeling is the warmth of soul; willing is the strength of
the depths. And you and I, all of us who live upon the
earth, particularly at Advent time, must know ourselves human, man, created in the true image of man,
because we have thinking, feeling and willing. Our
thinking, feeling and willing need the light of the

---

1. Matthew 24, verse 30.

heights, the warmth of soul, and the depths of will. If these become audible to us, something of this folk song sings in us and we feel ourselves a little more human in our loneliness. Advent can really become a kind of community festival, because with this kind of music we can meet properly without being just together in a heap and losing ourselves. We can recognize in each other the thinking, feeling and willing. We can recognize in each other that on the clouds of warmth, light and will, thinking, feeling and willing appear as the Son of Man in each one. The festival of Advent can become a true festival huddling around candles, but in the sense that His Advent can be expected in each one of us.

Certainly we must light the candle in ourselves, so as to feel that our thinking, feeling and willing is all the time requiring to be re-lit, and the wick of our ordinary self is stuck into it. This is nevertheless a matter for each one of us alone. But just as Felix Braun lit in my loneliness a candle by his being, by his recognition of my thinking, feeling and willing, so each one of us, when we come together in community, require that someone lights a candle for us. We must learn how to light a candle for someone else to make this a true community festival.

There is an old, lovely custom. It is the custom of playing Wichtel for one another. Now, what is a Wichtel? A Wichtel is a small being, maybe like a gnome, an elemental being whom nobody can really see because he is so quick and clever and at the same time always does the right thing. And the custom of playing the Wichtel for somebody else is, that each person, in the Advent time, "adopts" another person. It is not necessarily his best friend, often the opposite;

maybe somebody with whom one doesn't get on too well. Such a person is "adopted" and one plays Wichtel to him or to her. One tries, with tiny little deeds, to light a kind of friendly little candle for the other person. For instance, one has an apple or a tangerine, something precious that one wants to eat oneself. One wraps it up in a piece of paper and one places this tangerine under the pillow of that person. But one must not be seen and nobody must know who has put it there. It can be something quite small. It can be a lovely brown leaf that you have found on the ground, a little stone, and you place it there at least once a week, but maybe more often. And it needn't always be under the pillow. It can also be put, if nobody sees you doing it, into the other person's pocket. But you mustn't be discovered otherwise it is no "Wichtel" and everything is gone. Neither must you tell afterwards: "It was me." You must do it in secret and in secret light a candle for somebody else by doing a small good deed for him. That is one example of lighting a candle for somebody. Do a small deed that corresponds to lighting a candle for someone.

If you do that do you know what happens? The three lines of the folksong which I spoke to you become enlivened, because the thought of kindness for another person is an unselfish thought illumined by the highest. The warmth that you put into the little deed, the tangerine, the stone that you place unseen to give somebody a joy, is that which opens the eye of the soul, which gives warmth to the soul. To actually *do* it, not only want to do it, but actually do it when nobody sees you, for this you need your will. What we do in Advent, lighting candles for one another, enlivens in us the folksong for man on earth. Then, when

the time comes for our dying, we may expect the
"coming." For we shall be able to remember the Advent candles we lit for one another. We shall be able
after death to remember what we have thought in
this way, what the warmth of our soul has been preparing in this way, and what the depth of our will has
offered to someone else. And so Advent can become
a community festival.

Let me turn once more to my friend Felix
Braun. He knew that so well. I told you that I thought
he was the most Advent-like man that I have ever met.
In the whole way in which he related to people, in
which he related to the great poets, and to his friends,
and to those who had died and about whom he wrote,
in every way he was an Advent-man. And time and
again in the talks that he had with me there came up
the question: "What is it, really, that we can do which
we will remember when we have died?" I found
amongst his poems one with which I want to close tonight, because it expresses all this so beautifully. It is
in German but I have translated it for you. In it is
gathered up all I have tried to say tonight and with it
I would like to release you back into the further paths
of Advent with the hope that his Advent-words will be
with you and help you to go through this time. In German it is called "Besinnung im Damern":

Dass schon Laternen scheinen,
Fuhlst du vom Zwielicht her.
Dich drangt ein Damergrauen,
Vom Lesen aufzuschauen,
Das Herz ist dir, zum Weinen,
Von Trauerahnung schwer.

Festival Images for Today

Was sollen wir beginnen?
Zu kurz ist unsre Frist.
Wir kamen ungerufen
Und steigen Zeit wie Stufen
Bis zu den hochsten Zinnen,
Wo Nacht und Sternluft ist.

Einst werd auch ich dort stehen,
So jung ich heute bin.
Kein Fuhrer wird mich weisen,
Sternleuchten um mich kreisen,
Sternwinde um mich wehen—
Dann schwinde ich dahin.

Ach, liebes Herz, erwache!
Wir leben ja noch fort.
Sieh zu, dass auf der Erde
Ein freundlich Licht dir werde,
Wie ich es jetzt entfache
Aus dieser Lampe dort[1].

In English: "To ponder in the Twilight, in the Dusk."

That lamps already shine
You feel, because it's dusk;
Its graying urges on you
To look up from your book.
Your heart, as if in weeping
With sorrow heavy weighs.

---

1. From: Felix Braun, Viola d'Amore, Ausgewahlte Gedichte 1903-1953, Otto
Muller Verlag, Salzburg, 1953.

What shall we do or start now?
Too short is our span.
We came, not being bidden
And climb but time and steps
High to the battlements
Where night is, air of stars.

Once I will stand there also,
Howwever young I am.
No guide will lead me then.
Star-candles circling round me,
Star-winds will waft around me
Then will I wane away.

But, o my dear heart, waken!
We do yet still live on.
Watch, that upon this earth
A friendly light be yours,
Such as I try to kindle
Here now upon this lamp.

Advent
An Image for Our Time

Third Advent Sunday, 1969, Beaver Run, PA

Dear friends,

Entering into Advent time, I felt urged once again to review what Christmas and Advent mean for us. The many glories of the past which are for us a basically European tradition of Christmas celebrations, are, to me, ever less valid for everything that occurs in our time.

One begins to realize that it is one of the great losses for mankind to have lost the ability to celebrate festivals. A fundamental article about this appeared two weeks ago in the Saturday Review by a Harvard Professor who wrote about festivals and fantasy. He deplores the loss of what he calls one of the most human capacities, namely the capacity to celebrate festivals. They have been reduced to a meaningless repetition of outer things. He speaks of the truism that if one looks to so-called underdeveloped, primitive nations, their year seems to be punctuated by constant festivals, culminating in the great festivals of the year.

The spontaneous need and capacity to do that is almost gone from western life except in the most traditional sense. It is heartening to think that such things are spoken about increasingly by sociologists and anthropologists. For all of us the need for a full understanding, the eagerness to celebrate the festivals in a proper way, must be greater.

The festivals are the points from which we relate ourselves (or ought to relate ourselves) to the cosmos. I believe it would be a wonderful thing if we would say that in celebrating the festivals we try to be "Cosmonauts." We would then be relating ourselves to the cosmos, in contrast to those (while I wish in no way to diminish their feats) who try to find the cosmos with the same means by which after all we lost it.

The season that turns toward winter is one that should forcefully evoke in us a plan for what we are doing. At this time of the year, in turning inward and in reflecting, in having also a greater capacity to do so than in summer, we should perhaps even more consciously penetrate into the reasons for our celebrations.

For many of us the celebration of the festivals is increasingly related to the way in which we can—not only in pictures—but also with a certain amount of understanding, relate ourselves to the Christ as a Cosmic Being, as the Being of the Sun in its spiritual sense. We hope that by trying appropriately to celebrate festivals, people who feel less inclined to what Christianity may imply, may perhaps be able to feel the grandeur of the thought of the Christ and His Being which has for so long been fettered and clouded by the associations evoked by the churches and their theology.

In winter, when the sun becomes a rare visitor and when the glory of the Earth has disappeared, we know it has been inhaled by the being of the Earth. It is, so to speak, entirely within the earth. Then there arises a different possibility to look to the activity, the being and the effect of the cosmic, Spiritual Sun.

On Easter Sunday 1923[1], Rudolf Steiner spoke about the festivals. He mentioned a number of things which I will quote. Strongly calling upon his listeners he said: "Mankind must achieve an esoteric maturity in order to become again creative for festivals. Then mankind will again be able to relate the sequence of sense experience with the Spiritual." "It is today necessary for man to be able to do the esoteric." This is strongly expressed, but entirely in relation to what moves me. I am particularly concerned that a creative ability would come about, growing out of esoteric striving and background, which would be able to loosen our fantasy to such an extent that our fantasy forces would be in tune with the cosmic forces; that fantasy would, as it were, be cosmically informed and thereby able to create appropriate festivals.

There is an example of such a creative act done by a pupil of Rudolf Steiner's in which we can all participate every year with renewed wonder. This was the creation of the Advent-Garden by Dr. Karl Schubert. He is perhaps the greatest modern forerunner of

---

1. "The Cycle of the Year as a Breathing Process of the Earth and the Four Great Festivals." Five lectures, Dornach, Lecture 2, Easter Sunday, April 1, 1923.

those who will create truly spiritual festival images, through having related himself to the cosmic idea of the Advent-Garden.

Early on he was called by Rudolf Steiner to the Waldorf School in order to lead the first class for curative education. He was a wonderful, strong personality with tremendous powers of sympathy and love. A strange man at the same time, he remained a Roman Catholic all his life. Yet he was entirely devoted to Anthroposophy and to Rudolf Steiner. Through him the striving of curative education is linked with Waldorf education.

The image of the Advent-Garden is placed into a time when we normally assume that the rays of Michaelmas have disappeared. The Michaelmas time seems to have come to a certain end, also within the ritual of the Christian Community. The seasonal prayer begins again to change from the Michaelmas time into the Advent prayer, and one assumes that Advent is now a new experience, that Michaelmas is gone. But I believe we are justified in assuming that this is wrong.

In the same lectures to which I referred, Rudolf Steiner also speaks about this. "The Festival of Christmas is celebrated in a true way today when man understands that Michael has purified the earth so that at Christmas the birth of the Christ Impulse can happen in a right way," and "when man understands that today he has to add to this most mighty of pictures—that of the Christ arising from the tomb at Easter, conquering death, the picture that brings enlightenment into earth existence—to add to this the Being of Michael to the right of Jesus Christ permeating the earth's breathing power with the Christ-power during the cycle of one year of the earth's breathing process."

In greater detail Rudolf Steiner describes how Michael goes in front of Christ into earth existence. He cleanses with his rays of iron the atmosphere of the earth so that the Christ as the Spirit of the earth can be inhaled together with all the natural forces in Winter time. Michael precedes Him so that at Christmas time the earth can be permeated fully by the Christ Being and His forces. All the forces of earth are being christianized by the presence of the Christ within the earth and also Michael receives the blessing of this intimate presence. Then, again at the side of Christ-Jesus, he is exhaled by the earth when spring and summer come. He is totally renewed at the high point of summer by the cosmic forces, and refreshed at the time of St. John.

Thus we can learn in our time to look to the continued descent of the rays of Michael into the center of the earth, preceding and then side by side with the Earth-Spirit, with the Sun-Being of Christ. This takes place at that time of the year in which the words that resound throughout the earth are: "*Behold the evil.*" For during the time of mid-winter, the time of the winter of the earth, man must learn how to be inwardly prepared to face evil.

This seems to me perhaps the most important accent we can receive in our life: that in our social existence, striving inwardly and for one another, we must learn—in our time—to forge such human bonds and values that we are at the same time enabled to face evil. However, we do not only meet evil when winter comes, but our time is the Advent time of world evolution. And therefore Advent is not only an event within the breathing process of one year but Advent is the festival to prepare ourselves to be able to stand face to face with evil.

Advent time is not only this. Advent time is of course also the coming of the Son of Man in the clouds. In the course of one year Advent means to become inwardly prepared and ready to discern the Ether Christ at Christmas, the Son of Man in the glory of the rainbow.

Perhaps you have followed what is known in this country and in the world as the massacre of My Lai in Vietnam. Perhaps you have followed how a group of young American soldiers (average age 23) were involved in a way they themselves can hardly understand, in the kind of activity reminiscent of Auschwitz, Dachau, and Buchenwald. Here we have a fearful manifestation, an almost ununderstandable, incredible possession with evil. It is deeply puzzling even to these nice young men, the leader of whom, a lieutenant, was described by his teacher as a "typical nice American boy," helpful to his neighbors, kindly. He did not seem possessed, according to witnesses, when this massacre happened in Vietnam; possessed in the way people have been known to run amok when blood flows or in some action of mass hysteria. Neither were the other soldiers. But under circumstances, influenced of course, by the immense cruelty of this kind of war, they were shooting up anything—between a hundred and two hundred, some say five hundred civilians, mostly old men, women, children and babies. We may say: "Well, that has happened there." It hasn't happened there. It has happened in *our* body and in the body of mankind. All evil that occurs in the body of mankind is our own evil. We are not meant to regard evil as a psychedelic exercise that occurs to others. We are meant cosmically to learn to face it, and thereby perhaps to learn how one can resist it or redeem it. What happens when such a thing occurs? What kind of Advent breaks into the human soul?

In the lecture quoted earlier Rudolf Steiner describes something with the following words: "At wintertime we must learn to understand how the earth, because she is so thoroughly permeated by her soul and spirit, in these inner parts becomes particularly receptive to the effects of the moon forces. In ancient times the initiates told their pupils: There will come a time in the earth's evolution when the moon forces which are so strong in winter time will work so powerfully upon man that they will completely blot out men's awareness that they are spiritual beings. The time will come when the moon forces will take hold of men to such an extent that they will act throughout the whole year as if they would be guided by the moon forces."

Advent time is the time of our age. Advent time is a world preparation to understand this moment when the greatest light is within the earth: when the Sun, the Being of the Light, the Logos, the meaning, the soul and spirit of the earth is inhaled by the earth. In this time adversary moon forces of men are at work. The sun at midnight wants to shine as World-Christmas. We cannot behold it because we have largely lost any inkling that we are spiritual beings. And it is the moon that causes this.

How can we understand Hanukkah, the Jewish festival that is celebrated about the same time? It should continually be our question how the Christian festivals can be celebrated in the sense that Christ is understood as the fulfillment and meaning of the Earth, and so that the festivals of other religions have their place and order in it. Hanukkah is celebrated on the 25th day of Chislev of the Jewish year, which is usually our December. It celebrates a certain historic occasion which is well known and beautifully described in the first book of Maccabees.

After the breakup of the Hellenistic empire of Alexander the Great, the increasingly decadent kings of the East, amongst them the Syrian kings, the Selencids, started to exert complete and central power over all other peoples of the region. One of the most cruel was Antiochus IV, who called himself Epiphanes—"God-manifest." This happened in 175 B.C. He wanted to impose a totally perverted Hellenistic influence on all people over whom he ruled, amongst them Jews.

Together with a corrupt high priest of the Jews he established his definite rule also in Jerusalem. It is interesting that the high priest who cooperated with him had the name Jason. He subjugated the Jews to such an extent that he completely transformed their religious life, in the end forcing them to sacrifice pigs at the altar of the temple of Solomon, the High Temple in Jerusalem. It is said that gradually not only pigs but also human beings were sacrificed, all to "God-manifest," in the personality of Antiochus IV—Epiphanes. He robbed the temple treasure; he was what is called in the Jewish books "the abomination that makes desolate," and he finally evoked a strong underground resistance-movement amongst some religiously inspired Jews, particularly among the forerunners of the Essenes. The head of this was one Mattathias, an old man who had five sons. These five sons, whose leader was Judas, were then called the

Maccabees, which means "the hammers." The Maccabees finally defeated the army of the Syrian king and were able to create a sphere of peace around Jerusalem and in the Temple so that on the 25th day of the month of Chislev they could celebrate the feast of rededication of the altar, the re-kindling of the light.

This is celebrated today in a period of at least eight days, because the feast lasted eight days, whereby the Menorah, that is the ninefold candlestick of the Jews, is kindled in such a way that one candle is lit for every day. One candle gives the light for the next candle, so that for eight days it goes on until the ninefold Menorah is finally completely lit on the altar. This light of the Menorah is the rekindling of the light of the Sun on the altar of the temple. It is practically not known, (but it should be known) that the Maccabees were canonized in the early centuries by the Church. They were made Christian Saints. Hanukkah is in many ways reminiscent of the mood that you can sometimes find during the Advent-Garden. Hanukkah is, as it were, a way toward the light of the Sun in the ultimate Temple. It is also related to Lent. Indeed Advent is altogether related to Lent-time, not only by tradition, but by deep insight. On the first Advent Sunday we are reminded of Palm Sunday when we are celebrating the entry into Jerusalem.

The entry into Jerusalem is the occasion when Christ, the Being of the Sun, began to unify Himself completely with the body of Man, when he became one with the earth. But because all what is outside is also inside, this tremendous image of the entry into Jerusalem, the entry of the Being of the Sun riding on the donkey with the young colt running alongside, signifies the Sun within the human winter.

Where is the human winter? The human winter is the skeleton, the bones, the barren tree of the bones. The human winter is that which gives the structure to the otherwise constantly moving, changing, flexible constitution and body of the human being. The hardest part of the skeleton, the skull, is the polar-cap of our inner existence. Within this polar-cap there sits the moon landscape of our brain and the moon forces of our brain. The moon forces of our intellect have been touched for the first time by the Being of the Sun when He entered into the human body of Jesus and united Himself with it during the entry into Jerusalem.

We are often wrongly inclined to think that to be intellectual means to be intelligent. This does not need to be the case. If we would only recognize to what extent we are intellectual without being intelligent, it would be of tremendous help for the whole world! To look at the world in the way we do today, means to be intellectual, but by no means intelligent. Intellect can be understood as the reflective capacity that radiates, as if it were the moon itself, from the brain alone. But through the entrance of the Being of the Sun into the winter of man, something began to be constitutionally changed in man's body, which though it is initially related to the blood, has yet to do with a quite different part of the winter within man. Since Easter it began to change this "polar-cap." It began to melt the ice and started to establish a balance between the head pole and the rest of the body, in such a way that the part of man's winter which should be the true center was restored to him, namely his larynx. Through the entrance of the Word of the World, the Logos, into the human body, the larynx became the heart of the winter.

And now let us look for a moment again at the Advent-Garden. We know that there is the moss-spiral (wherever we can have moss), and in the center is perhaps a wooden trunk, and on the wooden trunk there stands a big light, a candle which is lit as the only light in the darkened room. At the entrance to the moss garden there are lying apples and in each apple there is a little candle. All around the moss garden here and there are glimmering jewels, are crystals and stones of all kinds. When the children come into the darkened room music is being played. Each one of the children, on behalf of all of us, in a kind of confession that reveals itself in their movements, takes up his own evil, his own apple, his own malum. He takes his own burden of evil and goes around this spiral to the central light and lights his own candle. Then he must make this all-important, all-revealing turn, must change around and go back again and then place his apple somewhere, anywhere along the way. His candle now stands anywhere he chooses, lit with the light from the central candle. The more children go, the lighter the room becomes through each individual deed. It is important that one imagines all this against the background of music. Each child should have the choice of a song of his own, his own song that accompanies him in and out of the spiral. The descent of light in this way has come to us as the creative deed of Karl Schubert.

This is the Advent-Garden. As we now look at it, and we certainly have done so many times, the all-important thing is that here—where the central light is to be met—a change can and should take place. The walk along the outer spiral into the world takes place.

Being able to place one's individual light along the way is now celebrated.

When seen from above, this is a world sign: it is the sign of Crab, or Cancer. The sign of Crab is the sign of every new beginning. It is the sign of the entry into Jerusalem, because the Sun stood in Crab when Christ rode into Jerusalem. It is also the sign in which the Sun stood when Jesus was born. Two of its stars are called "the two donkeys," "the two asses," but one of its major stars is called "the manger." The Crab is the sign of the coming of the Sun into the true manger, into the cradle of the earth, into the center of winter, riding on an ass and accompanied by a colt.

Dear friends, as an adult who unfortunately is no longer permitted to walk this spiral in celebration of the Advent-Garden festival, the Advent-Garden experience can be one of the greatest inner experiences leading toward Christmas. There is the immense expectation centering toward the light, being ever more burdened with the malum, the evil, the apple on the way to the center light. And there is the exvoluting spiral which becomes lit up by the lights of fellow human beings, in which the crystals shine in wonderful glory along this green path.

As an adult one begins to wonder how the experience of every child on the first of Advent as a new beginning could also be experienced by us older ones in such a way that this exvoluting spiral becomes the most important part of this image. This is the path that will lead to Christmas. It is the illuminating path becoming ever lighter as the other candles appear.

At the end there shines the star of Christmas like the holy host of angels that appeared to the

Shepherds. This light appearing at the end of the path, toward which we walk, this light of the Shepherds—what was it? That was the light that shone from the spirit body of the Buddha, the Nirmanakaya of the Buddha. It is a Buddha path, it is the eightfold path that guides us as adults through the Advent time of every year and through the Advent time of world evolution. It is the Crab path, related to the sense-organ of the Word, the sense-organ of the 16-petalled lotus flower, the sense-organ that is achieved by walking this path. It is the sense-organ that leads us toward preparing the cradle for the World Word. And it is also the rainbow path, because it is lit up by the descending rays of Michael, a rainbow over which the Sun-Chariot of the Being of the Sun travels into the earth.

In 1904[1], Rudolf Steiner gave a lecture on the light at Christmas, on the birth of the light. It is the only time, to my knowledge, that he spoke about Advent. It is in the same lecture that he also speaks about the sign of Crab. He speaks about the birth of the light in such a way that he leads us to understand the seven stages of initiation, the stages we have often, and yet never enough, dwelt upon, the stages that belong to the occult traditions of all mankind, irrespective of creed, religion or country. These seven stages, as you know are: One—the Raven, the one who begins to be a messenger between what is spoken of as "spiritual light" and the earth. The second stage is that of the Occult One, who can dwell freely in both spheres, in the heights as well as on the earth. The

---

1. Berlin, December 19, 1904, 1st of 3 lectures. "Zeichen und Symbole des Weihnachtsfestes."

Third stage of initiation is the Fighter, who can now stand up prepared and who is called upon to fight for spiritual truths. The Fourth is the Lion, and the Fifth he who has gathered up in himself the soul of the people to which he belongs, he may be called the Persian, or the Israelite, or according to where-so-ever he was. The Sixth is the Sun-Hero, and the Seventh can belong to the sphere of the Fathers. It is a humbling thought that in our time we are already meant to prepare in general for the seventh stage, not fit to reach it, but to prepare for it. When Rudolf Steiner speaks about this he says the following: "The fifth cultural epoch which prepares a point of time that has to come, will have to bring to us the belief in the new initiates, the Fathers. Those initiated in the seventh degree are called the Fathers. We speak in the spiritual-scientific world conception and in its language about the knowledge of the Masters. For there is not only one, but there are more Masters to whom man looks upward in gratitude and devotion as to the great leaders of mankind. In this way we will be able to connect the fifth cultural epoch with our future. So it seems to us as we look to the fourth cultural epoch to see it placed into the midst of a very great process through which we go, the process of Advent, which actually means three epochs that have passed. The three weeks of Advent are an image for these, because man must recapitulate in himself these three stages, as when in earlier times one celebrated the arising of the light at Christmas time. Only then can follow the life in the light—"das Leben im Lichte." Therefore the Christmas festival is for the Christian not something that passes, not merely a memory of something that has passed. In the Christmas song it does not say

"Christ has been born," or "Christ was born," but it says: "today Christ is born." This is important and significant. It is spoken of today in the sense in which Christ Himself spoke: "I am with you until the end of the days." That is what stands before us every year anew and reveals to us the relation of man and the heavens. He showed us that there must take place in man that which has already taken place in the heavens. And as the Sun cannot leave her course by one centimeter without causing confusion, so also must man keep to his path. He must achieve that inner harmony and that inner rhythm, which present to him the experience of Christ, who was incarnated in that Jesus who will work amongst the Fathers, to whose guidance man must experience himself as belonging in the future times."

Who are the Fathers? "The Fathers of harmony and of the concord of mutual feeling," Rudolf Steiner called them with an older description. Who are they? The Fathers have also sometimes been called the seven Rishis. Their seat, their spiritual domicile is on the moon. To obtain an inkling of the Fathers today means to prepare oneself inwardly to meet the forces of the inner moon, inside and outside. It also means to learn to be able to withstand what as sheer evil is at work in the body of mankind. None of those young Americans who were present at the massacre in Vietnam had any certainty within themselves concerning the Fathers, or through them to the Father-God within themselves. They belong to the increasing generations of the cosmically ill. Not to be able to lift oneself up inwardly to the Father means to be ill because of the negative moon forces active within oneself. Thus Advent and Christmas may be experienced as a festival of the light of the Fathers which begins to shine upon earth, as a preparation for finding the Fathers again today as the spiritual guides of mankind.

We can learn to practice for it, I think, if unafraid and certain within ourselves, we are willing to go the path that prepares us for winter. As I close, and on the basis of these pictures laid before us through Rudolf Steiner's words, there is yet one more picture that we will perhaps see arising from our inner activity. We can see lying there—as we behold the Advent-Garden, as we build it up, either outside ourselves in a Hall or inside ourselves, in our soul as an exercise, the green snake which has sacrificed itself in order to become the rainbow bridge, glistening as with thousands of jewels. And on one side arises the Temple where the three Kings stand, the Gold, the Silver and the Copper Kings, representatives of the three epochs which have passed. But the fourth King, the mixed one, which is the representative of our time, has crumbled away. From the other side, people begin at long last to walk over this bridge toward the Temple, people of all nations, of all religions, of all kinds, because they themselves have become aware of the first inkling of light, and that the Fathers are again alive in us. This image of the Fairy-tale by Goethe tells us what Advent must be: the true entry into our time. We can see that these images that have been created out of Advent or that point toward Advent enable each one of us to enter into our time better prepared. If we do not enter into our time well prepared there will be no Christmas. We may feel this tremendous urge not to omit anything we can do, so that Christmas can be. To celebrate Advent

with these images must become for us and others a
need, a cosmic necessity in which we can help each
other, in which we can take each other by the hand
as we move across this bridge, but in which we also
must learn to acknowledge the light of the Fathers
shining through the three Kings in the Temple.

Three Meetings of the Soul
(A Christmas Address)

January 3, 1975, Beaver Run, PA

"To become aware of the idea within
reality is the true communion of Man. "
— RUDOLF STEINER

My friends,

We have had a remarkable few days together under this image of the tree, which since it was introduced as one of the archetypal images of mankind, not more than 150-200 years ago, has increasingly become an image for the tree of life. At Christmas our longing goes to the tree of life and to it I want to direct my words.

It is one of the aspects of the arrogance that can occur in the pursuit of spiritual activity to believe that one can dispense with religion when one "has" meditation. This arrogance is unfortunately widespread. I would like to place before us a few words which Steiner said in a lecture given in Berlin, February 20, 1917, called "The Human Soul and the Universe"[1]. This lecture is the basis of more or less all I say tonight, and I would like to duly acknowledge the copyright herewith! "One should never represent spiritual scientific activity as if it could be a substitute for religious exercises or for religious life. Spiritual science can in the highest degree be an underpinning of religious life in particular with regard to the Christ-Mystery and it can be an underpinning of religious exercises. One shall not *make* religion with spiritual science, but one shall be clear enough about the fact that religion in its living life, as a living exercise within a human community enkindles the spirit-consciousness of the soul. If this spirit-consciousness is to become a living thing in man, he cannot remain within the abstract concepts of God or of Christ, but must ever anew take it up into his religious exercising, into his religious activity. This activity certainly can take on many different forms for different people but man must stand in something which surrounds him like a religious milieu; he must stand in something that speaks to him as religious environment. And if this religious milieu is deep enough, if this religious environment can sufficiently stimulate the soul, then the soul will feel a longing toward concepts—will just *then* feel longing for concepts—that are developed in and through spiritual science. In an objective sense spiritual science is most certainly a support for religious attempts to lift oneself up. And

---

1. "Cosmic and Human Metamorphoses"—Berlin, 7 Lectures. Anthroposophical Publishing Co. London, (no year). Lecture 3: The Human Soul and the Universe, Berlin, February 20, 1917.

today the time has come of which we have to say that
a religiously feeling human being will be driven by
his feeling also to want to *know*. For in religious feeling arises today of necessity a spirit-consciousness. In
the same way in which knowledge of nature arises
within natural science, so within spiritual science
spirit-consciousness leads to the urge to gain knowledge of the Spirit. One can say objectively that it is
just through strongly inward religious life that today
human beings can be led to Spiritual Science"[1].

I am reminded of the phrase: "The Spirit is willing
but the flesh is weak." We are reminded of this fact:
what we can say to each other, what we can quote to
each other, what we can attempt to learn in thought,
many a time convinces us of the Spirit. But our flesh
is weak. Not only do we forget it again but we can't
live up to what we *know*. Of course we can't. But even
more, it means that out of that "flesh" we cannot yet
draw the resources to think for ourselves what we
thought through the help of others, feel what we felt
through such thoughts and, least of all, will what
ought to be willed as a result. And yet I also felt—as
perhaps a good number of you have—that our Christmas festival was an attempt to provide a basis on
which to develop the fundaments of a spiritual community like ours, that fundament in particular on
which alone the Fundamental Social Law can live. It
was an attempt to regain and to live for a time in a
uniting world-view, a spirit-view of the world. Without
this, neither we nor any other group of people can
succeed socially in community life and least of all with

---

1. This is possibly a foreword contained in original German edition, translated
by Carlo. Not contained in the English publication.

an economic-social striving in which egoism shall not kill all that has been attempted.

Let us be reminded how Rudolf Steiner, after he had given "The Fundamental Social Law" described this fundament. In his essays "Anthroposophy and the Social Question" (1905-06)[1] he says that the Fundamental Social Law cannot succeed unless another condition is also fulfilled. Even those who try to work not for reward but who seek in the other one the purpose of this work, even these will be overwhelmed by egoism unless another condition is also fulfilled. "There is only one thing which can be of any use; and that is a spiritual world-conception, which of its own nature, through what it has to offer, can find a living abode in the thoughts, in the feelings, in the will—in man's whole soul, in short. That faith which Owen had in the goodness of human nature is only true in part; in part, it is one of the worst of illusions. It is true to the extent that in every human being there slumbers a "higher self" which can be awakened. But the bonds of its sleep can only be dispelled by a world-conception of the kind described. One may induce men, then, into conditions such as Owen devised, and the community will prosper in the highest and fairest sense. But if one brings men together, without their having a world-conception of this kind, then all that is good in such institutions will, sooner or later, inevitably turn to bad. With people who have no world-conception centered in the spirit it is inevitable that just those institutions which promote men's material well-being will have the effect of also enhancing

---

1. "Anthroposophy and the Social Question," 3 Essays, 1905-06. Rudolf Steiner Mercury Press, Spring Valley, 1982.

egoism, and therewith, little by little, will engender want, poverty, and suffering. For it may truly be said, in the simplest and most literal sense of the word: An individual man you may help by simply supplying him with bread; a community you can only supply with bread by assisting it to a world-conception of the spirit. Nor indeed would it be of any use to try and supply each individual member of the community with bread since, after a while, things would still take such a form that many would again be breadless"[1].

We must bear in mind the essential fact of uniting in a spiritual world-view. We must turn to it not only because one understands but also because one experiences and knows that this is true. We must turn time and again to an effort in common experience, not only because somebody leads, but because of the common experience of renewing the awareness of this uniting Spirit-concept.

I now must turn to the religious atmosphere in which this took place, when it became real for us. We must turn to the slumbering self. I believe, in turning to the blue of heaven, we first must turn to the sleeping human being. What we are asked is to be aware not only of the call that is going out constantly to us, as it has done for thousands of years: "O man, know yourself," but also of this call: "O man, know your sleeping self." I wish to turn for a short while to the sleeping self in which we submerge ourselves night by night. I want to turn to the night in each one of us, to the night of the year also, and thus toward the Sun at

1. Ibid, pg. 27-28. Robert Owen 1771-1858, English social reformer—"A genius of practical social work." He created a model of modern community in Indiana, N.A. (1824).

midnight, toward the light that shines out of darkness. I will recall first of all the three steps in which we tried to understand ourselves throughout the last few days; the step of *wonder*, the step of *compassion*, and the step of *conscience.*

As we think of wonder, we allow ourselves to *be* turned by our sense of wonder—in the words of the beautiful poem by Andrew[1]—from the "thankful nature of yellow, to the blue of heaven." We begin by allowing ourselves to wonder about the starry sky, about the heavens from which these incredible forms and configurations shine upon us as they have done for millennia. We begin by unfolding our wonder at the hand of the stars. The question that can arise within us when we do it could well be: "What stirs in us when wonder reaches out to the stars?"

Then we turn to compassion: compassion, that field of experience when we encompass a thing, a being, a situation, a person. We encompass what we encounter when we not only stare and look, but when we begin to pass into the object that is now no longer quite object(ive), and the object passes into us. We encompass it when we begin to read the phenomena we observe as if they would now be able to say something new and unheard of; as if we would begin to decipher the hidden writing of their appearance, to become one to the extent of becoming newly aware of it, not only its appearance. The question may arise: "Whence do we receive this power of uniting?"

Then we go to the third experience and recall aspects of conscience. Conscience is no longer a reading

---

1. The poem is reproduced at the end of the lecture. Andrew Hoy is a poet and long-time Camphill co-worker, presently living in Camphill Village, Copake, N.Y.

of that which is conveyed to us by the power of compassion. It sets us in motion because we can hear something spoken to us, the call of action. We begin to hear what we have encompassed, the idea speaks to us out of that which we have encompassed. Then we begin to *divine*, to feel the Divinity in what we are encompassing. A will begins to stir in us which is not only our own. With the voice of conscience there stir the beginnings of a moral will. The will of the world begins to move in us for a higher purpose. The question arising is: "Who is the source of this?"

Rudolf Steiner speaks about this in the lecture that I mentioned to you before: "The Human Soul and the Universe." He speaks about three meetings of the human soul with the beings of the Universe, three meetings that take place during our sleep, in our unconsciousness. Through these three meetings we are enabled to weave—when we are awake—on the three garments of which we have spoken, the three garments of the soul that we call wonder, compassion and conscience. These three meetings enable us to weave these three garments and we receive them as an always renewed gift in our sleep. They are capacities that, inasmuch as they are able to work into our wakeful existence, enable us to weave these garments. These meetings relate to what took place long before the Mystery of Golgotha as the three pre-earthly deeds of the Christ—when the Christ intervened three times in the evolution of man. When the harmonious becoming of man was threatened by deterioration He brought about at first the healing of the senses; secondly, the healing of the life-processes and thirdly, a balancing of the powers of the soul. These deeds seem to be renewed, repeated, lifted up in an ongoing evolution but without us knowing about them when we are asleep, when we are unaware. The first of these three meetings takes place for the individual human being every night. I don't think one can improve on the urgency and earnestness with which Dr. König many, many times described how important it would be, for those who incarnate into our time, to learn to sleep, to learn to sleep so that not mere mindlessness overtakes us, but that we can keep a thread of *heart-awareness* from the moment of falling asleep to the moment of waking up. Whatever time we are allotted to sleep by our Karma, by our constitution, our disposition, the circumstances,—in the middle of our deep sleep, in the middle of our falling into unconsciousness we meet with our Angelos, with our angel, our genius. We meet with what is called our own Manas, our Spirit-Self; that part of our astral existence into which our Self has been able to work during the day, our Manas-Angelos. Through this meeting we carry into our waking life the *wonder* about the Spirit in every thing. The echo of this meeting is such that in us can arise the wonder we feel about how every thing and every being is *more* than that which we usually perceive. Through this meeting a kind of etherization of our senses takes place. Through this meeting we are sensitized to be able to follow up wonder with such inner attention that we can begin to receive back into us, from what we see and observe, something of the spiritual reality of what we have seen. Our spiritual understanding is fructified through it. It takes place in our head activity. It enlivens the ether body of our head. It makes us, quite differently now, the owner of this image of the dome of heaven that we carry as our heads. It crowns us with what has been given to us through our senses.

Rudolf Steiner described this meeting in the following way: "Man can experience in the middle of a longer period of sleep that which one must call an intimate living together with his Spirit-Self, that is, with the spiritual qualities out of which his Spirit-Self will have developed his meeting with his genius. This meeting with his genius, his Angelos, takes place every night or within every long period of sleep and it is immensely important to the human being. Whatever feeling of satisfaction we may have with respect to our relationship with the spiritual world, is dependent on the fact that this meeting during sleep echoes on— this meeting with the angel. The feeling that we can gain in our wakeful condition a relationship with the spiritual world is an after effect of our meeting with the angel every night"[1].

Dear friends, we can still have an inkling of this more easily than with the other two meetings. It was readily discernible to earlier men. The harmonious structuring of the ether-head is strengthened through the echoing awareness of that first meeting. This is present, active and in movement, for instance when we meet each other. When two people meet and dislike each other, which I understand happens from time to time, their ether-heads bend towards each other like in an "E-vo-e"; when they love each other, which also happens, the ether-head goes back and radiates from the hindhead. The purer this is and the less bound to human earthly relationship only, the more this radiation became visible in the past. It

---

1. Ibid—Pg. 25 (free rendering by Carlo).

was painted as the aura, or the gloria, that was depicted around the head of saints. Some of these wonderful images of crowns that kings wore are related to that gold that appears in the etherbody, echoing the meeting with the Angelos.

The second meeting takes place over a much wider time-space. This meeting, in quite unconscious depths, takes place for every human soul at Christmas time. It unfolds in the course of the year, beginning at Christmastime, particularly following the Christmas festival and unfolding night by night even when we have only an inkling of that which in the course of the year moves in and through us. Even though we can be free from the compulsion of the course of the year, when we meet with that Christmas activity taking place in the surrounding of the earth and within the earth itself, when the spirit of the earth draws most deeply inward and we can go with it—a Christmas meeting takes place with an Archangelic being. Through the forces of this Being our Self begins to work on the ether-body, developing the Buddhi, the Lebensgeist, the Life-Spirit. This constitutes a meeting, through the vehicle of an Archangelic being, with the Christ.

Every Christmas, at the midnight hour of the year, we meet in our sleep and in unconsciousness through the forces of an archangelic being with the Being of the Christ. This meeting wishes to become ever more conscious to us as the year proceeds, culminating in Easter. Please understand, the words are carefully chosen: it *wishes to become conscious to us,* to re-echo in our consciousness at Easter. It reaches another culmination at the time of St. John's when our being is drawn out, together with the elemental world from

the earth, and meets in the heights the manifesta-
tions of the World-Word.

In this meeting at Christmas time, the etherization of our blood meets with the etherization of the
aura of the earth. This is the leading together of our
blood and its impure gold with the forces of the being
of Christ who has since the Mystery of Golgotha irradiated the aura of the earth. During the day this enlivens in us our heart activity. Heart and lung begin to
pulsate in the re-echoing of what happened during
sleep. Let me read again the words of Rudolf Steiner
as he describes this second meeting: "It is this specific
feeling which we unite with the Christmas-mystery,
with the festival of Christmas and by no means is it
something arbitrary. It is related even with the fixing
of that festival to a certain point in time. In the winter
days in which this festival takes place man indeed is
given up to the spirit. Man really lives in a kingdom
where the spirit stands close to him. And the consequence of this is that right around the Christmastime,
up to our present New Year's night and so on, in this
time, the human being undergoes a meeting of his astral body with the Life-Spirit during sleep in the way
which was described in the first meeting. It is the
meeting of the Ego with the Spirit year. From this
meeting with the Life-Spirit, there grows the feeling
to be near to the Christ Jesus. For through the Buddhi, through the Life-Spirit, the Christ Jesus reveals
Himself. He reveals himself through a being of the
kingdom of the Archangeloi. Naturally, he himself is
an infinitely higher being. What now matters is that in
this meeting He reveals Himself through a being of
the kingdom of the Archangeloi. Thus through this
meeting, in present day evolution since the Mystery of

Golgotha, we stand particularly close to the Christ Jesus by having this meeting of the Life-Spirit in the deepest depth of our soul. The human being, for the development of his spirit consciousness, particularly in the sphere of religious feeling and of religious exercises can supplement this, can add to it the concepts received through spiritual science. Thus the human being deepens his feeling life, spiritualizes it in the way described and thus he will be able to experience also in waking life the after-echo of the meeting with the Spirit-Self, which means: with the Christ"[1]. The etherization which takes place in this meeting bestows upon us—within the circulation of our etherized blood—a spirit sheath, a cloak that we gradually begin to wear, constantly renewed, re-woven, in our circulation.

The third meeting takes place in a still wider context, also in total unconsciousness. It occurs at the midpoint of life between the years 28 and 42. For somebody who has the karma to die earlier, this meeting is condensed into the hour of his death. In this meeting we are led through the powers of an Archai, to the powers of the Father-God as represented in Spirit-Man, in Atman, in that part of our being in which our Ego has been working into the physical body. Through this meeting a kind of etherization takes place, via the powers of the blood, of our will and something of the etherized will of the world begins to re-echo within our will, within our acts of will, of our activity. The doing of the good is now no longer feeling but can flow into our actions. We receive the golden shoes with which we can walk into our

1. Ibid—Pg. 26 (free rendering).

Karma, becoming a servant of the golden globe which we hold in our kingly hands to fulfill our destiny upon the christened earth.

What I wanted to suggest at hand of these three descriptions is: Behold, in sleep we are Kings! When we are asleep we are crowned by the meeting with the Angelos. We receive our cloak through the meeting with the Archangelos who carries with him the being of Christ. We receive the golden shoes or the golden globe in the meeting with the Archai. We lie, sleeping kings, on the bed of our lives. In our waking days we are, as we know, stumbling creatures, and whether we are called Ulysses or Holy Smoke or incensed Frank [1] makes little difference! But you see, what we *can* do—and I believe it is possible to feel that it is attainable when we meet under the Christmas tree—is to become Shepherds during the day and go in search of the Child. It is possible to learn during the day to work together with other shepherds involved in the same mystery: the Mysterium Magnum of Golgotha. It is the same mystery that has redeemed the earth and has redeemed the human being and through him may redeem Lucifer.

What we have done is such an attempt, through subjecting ourselves as a community from time to time intensively, to re-echoing our sleeping being into our day. That which has taken place during these festival days was an alchymical process of the community which, if it can understand itself rightly, is engaged in an attempt to distill and offer gold. The reason for this is ultimately that we may learn to work

---

1. Names refer to characters in "The Female and the Fool", a play by Carlo Pietzner.

with, that we may learn to have devotion for and that
we may ultimately be able to behold the Trinity; the
Trinity which is the idea within and behind the Universe of our world. This three-foldness-giving Trinity
we can begin to worship through a common effort, a
common experience, a common resolve of goodwill.
And then we can say, as the Speaker does at the end
of the play[1]: "Even though the Spirit wills and the
flesh is weak, the Spirit lives." The Spirit lives indeed!
To behold even a glimpse of the idea of the Universe
is to worship the Trinity, and inspires us to a constantly renewed community effort.

A Harvest Poem

I did not know that yellow
Had a thankful nature
Yet when the barley ends
Its greenish dreams and burns
With golden flame it turns
My eyes away and up
Into the blue of heaven.

— ANDREW HOY

---

1. The Female and the Fool

112

Image and Reality
in Relation to the Christmas Tree

Third Advent Sunday, 1968, Beaver Run, PA

Dear Friends:

Tonight I would like to talk about Image and Reality. I would like to talk about it in relation to the Christmas tree.

All who have not an entirely veiled soul must be in one way or another deeply moved to see the Paradise Play. It is such a simple play and of such great impact that it really cannot fail to reach into the depth of one's being. One realizes that even the simplest lines reach to the very ground of existence. I am sure that is something we all share and I would hope in varying degrees could be shared with almost anybody who sees the play.

The play uses a tree, the Tree of Knowledge of good and evil, as one of its major images. We have often spoken about it and its relationship to the Christmas tree, the image of the Tree of Life. In some ways one may feel that the moment the Paradise play has been performed, or the images of Creation have again risen up and resounded in one's soul, Christmas in the more specific sense of the word, has begun.

Christmas really begins with this image of the Creation. This is one of the oldest, perhaps *the* oldest, origin of Christmas. We are reminded -as the basis of one's Christmas preparation—of the Creation and of the creatures who are both the crown of the Creation and those who abused the gifts with which they were endowed. And we are all more familiar with the Fall than we dare to acknowledge. It is with us as a constant certainty from morning until night, whether we hide it in our unconsciousness or not. In this sphere of Christmas (with these thunderous motifs of the Creation and the Fall), it is a most interesting thing to recall the themes about which Rudolf Steiner spoke over many years concerning Christmas.

In these lectures and among these motifs Rudolf Steiner has often spoken about the Christmas tree— the Christmas tree as a symbol. There also exists a lecture by him which bears this title[1].

There are three guiding lines which particularly spoke to me out of these many lectures; and all these occurred in lectures which Rudolf Steiner gave in Berlin. His first lecture "The Christmas Tree a Symbol"—was given on the 21st December, 1909. He tries to make his listeners aware of the fact that one can do something with the Christmas tree as a symbolum. One shall not leave it as an outer symbolum for Christmas, because it could be the image of

---

1. "The Christmas Tree, a Symbol." Dec. 21, 1909—"*The Festivals of the Season.*" Early edition in English translation. Out of print since 1930.

something extraordinarily significant and important. He speaks about the history of the Christmas
tree as part of the Christmas-festival repeatedly in
the course of the lecture: "Then we look", he says "at
this outer symbolum which we have standing before
us as the Christmas tree and we may say to ourselves:
it should become for us a symbolum that in our soul
should shine and burn"[1]. And then he says quite
clearly: "Thus Anthroposophy as it spreads by and
by, warming and enlightening the hearts and souls
of men of the present day and of the future may
transform into gold the materialistic outer use of the
Christmas-tree"[2]. Anthroposophy must make gold
out of the tree, penetrate it with its wisdom and
make it into an important, golden symbol. After the
tree rose out of the dark foundations of the soul in
the course of the most recent times, it has made its
entrance into the light of the earth.

This becomes interesting on the basis of what we
tried to find out about our own Christmas. I thought
again about something that you will probably readily
recall, as I have often spoken about it as a recurring
theme for myself; namely that to a certain extent we
ought to feel like conspirators, like people who are
bound into a conspiracy, a conspiracy to serve the
Spirit in a world which believes to be much more real
than the world that we try to build up and in which we
believe. No time has been more urgently impressing
this on me than now.

Perhaps we are not content with the fact that we
operate to a certain extent "illegally," if you under-

1. Ibid.
2. Ibid.

stand what I mean: illegally—that is, to a certain extent against the currents of our time. We try to do it with a certain amount of stubbornness, to which we faithfully keep. We feel that unless we take upon ourselves the oddness and also painful consequences that it sometimes has, we will not, I believe, be able to serve what is spiritually true. The time is here to be serious about the Spirit!

This is not an unrelated remark, dear friends, to what I am trying to develop tonight, for in trying to serve the Spirit, we have to choose certain paths. We have to pursue specific methods. Such methods are difficult to outline with a few words. But at the moment it is the method of the image. It is an attempt to relate oneself with such inner sensitivity, surety and stillness to certain images, that what is to be served spiritually can become tangible. To a certain extent this method implies the weakness of our position, because contrary to the definite guidelines of life, we can rarely proceed without a good deal of careful weighing up and even faltering. The Spirit is not readily accessible. Of course this fact is often used as a reproach by many people. They easily say: "Why do you have to explain so much, why is everything so complicated?"

It belongs to the core of our subject to have to point out that if it would be possible to have "ready access" to the Spirit, to know easily what is right, to be able always to direct oneself according to "principles", just then all this would *not* be according to the Spirit. Just as it has not been possible for man to look the sun in the face, it is not possible for the human soul to be able to confront the Spirit directly. The moment the human being is confronted directly with the

Spirit, without long and arduous preparation, his life is extinguished.

Our one difficulty is therefore in trying to preserve the direction towards the reality of the Spirit, not to look the Sun in the face. Man will not be able, perhaps not for a long time, to look into the face of the Spirit without an image, without a semblance or picture. This can of course also be at times a word or a verse where the word assumes an image-quality.

It is not possible for man on earth to relate himself to the Spirit without this veil or image or parable in which it manifests itself—without being consumed. It is for that reason that even the Christ had to speak in parables to his disciples, except for the 40 days. Therefore it requires a kind of faithfulness and perseverance not to lose the certainty of the Spirit. We must look for it in images.

If we describe it in this way it does however not follow that the everyday world is therefore more real, or what we call more real. True it is that the everyday world is infinitely more confusing. It is real in the sense that it has a self-propelling power which makes us believe that we are in it, in reality. It seizes and takes hold of us without allowing us the possibility to step back, to gain consciousness and deliberate as we can with an image.

I wish we would have a long time together and that we could go into all kinds of directions. One of the reasons why I wish this now is that I would dearly love to read a long part from the second part of Faust. If one lives into these verses, a mood is created with such immense grandeur and beauty that, merely submerging oneself in it, is sufficient to know what one really means by image and reality.

However, I will only quote the very end of it. It is this marvelous part when Faust wakes up again and begins to speak about the deep inside knowledge of himself, about the existence of man, feeling himself to be a representative of man in this moment, within the circle of nature; " . . . The Sun appears and already in this very moment I am blinded, and turn away, penetrated with the pain of the light"[1]. In the énd he says: "Thus shall the sun remain at my back. The falling waters, rustling through the mountain rocks—I behold them with growing delight. From cliff to cliff they fall in thousand and many thousand streams, high into the air, lifting up foam upon foam—Alone how beautiful there springs from this storm, arching itself—the beautiful colored arc, sometimes clearly designed, sometimes dissolving in air, around itself spreading cool shivers of air and scent. This arc—it mirrors the human endeavour: Think about it and you will understand more clearly: in the colorful image you have life"[2].

The rainbow is the image of life. But life is being destroyed when it faces the light directly, the light of the Spirit. Life as we know it is intertwined with knowledge. It is inseparable from knowledge. Here we shall turn toward the Golden Legend, which Rudolf Steiner takes up a number of times when he speaks about Christmas, because this legend describes in an image the reality of the intertwining of life and knowledge. I only need to describe it very briefly. It is said that Seth—the son of Adam and Eve, who was born after Cain and Abel's encounter—is allowed to return to Paradise. There he receives per-

1. Faust, Second Part—Act I, Scene I, Johann Wolfgang von Goethe.
2. Ibid.

mission from Michael to take three seeds from the
Tree of Life with him. As he returns to his Father's
dwelling on earth, he carries these three seeds of the
Tree of Life with him and when his Father Adam has
died, Seth places him in a tomb and he plants the
three seeds into the mouth of his dead father and
buries him in a cave. From this cave there begin to
grow two trees which are entwined like a braid of hair:
The Tree of Knowledge and the Tree of Life—the
one growing directly out of the body of Adam, the
other one from the three seeds of the Tree of Life. Intertwined they grow out of his tomb. From the wood
of these two trees, which are intertwined, was carved
the staff of Moses with which he called forth the waters; out of this wood was carved the door to the Temple of Solomon; the trunk of the tree was ordered by
Solomon to be laid over the water that hindered the
Queen of Sheba from entering the Temple of Solomon, so that she—as over a bridge—might come
with dry feet into the Holiest of Holies. But this wood
was lying in this pool of water; the pool remained
throughout the ages and it became the pool of Be-
thesda, the healing pool of the time of Christ. But the
trunk also was the one out of which the cross was
made on which on Golgotha the Christ was nailed.

Now as I said this legend which you can read in
various versions belongs to the oldest legends that
have been found in manuscripts in the East, particularly in Ethiopia. Rudolf Steiner quotes it in a lecture
from Berlin 17th December 1906,—called "Signs
and Symbols of the Christmas Festival"[1]. It is in this

---

1. *The Festivals and their Meaning*, Vol. I Christmas, 17th Dec. 1906, Berlin. English publication 1967, Rudolf Steiner Press, London.

lecture, as he gathers this legend up, that we begin to understand the wonderful words: "Knowledge can be gained only at the cost of life."

Dear friends, I am not attempting to interpret this statement, but I would rather place it like a yoke upon our hearts, because it is good if we question ourselves to what extent are we willing to accept this to be true. To what extent are we still living in the illusion that what real knowledge we may have could be gained without losing something of one's life in exchange for it? This question of truth and reality belongs to the innermost message of Christmas.

The use of the Tree of Knowledge means our capacity to really be able to judge, but not in the usual sense. It means to make gains in the search of the age-old approach towards the understanding of man, as it was written above the mystery temples: "Man, know thyself." That is the kind of knowledge which is meant here. This real knowledge of reality is precisely the moment in which reality and image become one. How they become one is also described in a most wonderful way by Rudolf Steiner in yet another lecture, given in Berlin 19th December, 1915, a lecture called "The Christmas Thought and the Secret of the Ego," with the subtitle "The Tree of the Cross and the Golden Legend"[1]. Rudolf Steiner says: "There grows the Tree, the Tree which becomes the cross of the earth existence, the cross. The Tree becomes that to which men must gain a new relationship. For the old relationship made this Tree to grow—the Tree of the cross, that cross which grows from the earth evolution, that has been impinged upon by Lucifer. This

---

1. "*Der Weihnachtsgedanke und das Geheimmis des Ich*"—(no English publication).

Tree of the Cross grows out of Adam's tomb—out of that humanity which has become humanity after Adam, who has succumbed to the temptation. The Tree of Knowledge must become the stem of the cross because with the properly recognized Tree of Knowledge man must unite himself anew in order to achieve the good, the task of the earth. If we ask ourselves—and here we touch upon a most significant secret of Spiritual Science: "How is it actually with the members of human nature about which we have heard so much?" Then we will say, of course: "Everyone knows the first, the highest, member of human nature is our ego. We learn to say "I" at a certain moment in our childhood. We gain a relationship to this ego from the time which we can in later age only just still remember. We know from the various spiritual scientific observations what the ego has been doing until that moment which we can remember and when we began to say "I" to ourselves. The ego has itself been forming and shaping us, working on us, on ourselves, up to the moment where we gain a conscious relationship to our ego by saying "I." In a small child this ego is also there but it works in it—it forms the body. Before that it works as a supersensible power of the Spiritual world. When we have passed through conception and birth, it works in our body until we have formed our body to such a tool that we can consciously take hold of it, i.e. our ego.

But there is a deep secret connected with the ego entering into the human body. We ask when we meet a man: "How old are you?" He says the age according to the years that have passed since his birth. As I said, we are touching here a definite secret of Spiritual Science, which should become ever more clear to us in the course of the studies of the next years, which I would want to convey to you, make it known to you. What the man says is his age is merely related to his physical body. He says nothing else than that his physical body has been for such and such a time in evolution since his birth. The ego does not undergo any of this evolution, the ego remains behind—the ego never becomes older than 3 years. ["Und das ist das schwer zu fassende Geheimnis. . ."]—that is the difficult to grasp secret, that the ego actually remains behind at that moment of time up to where we can remember it. It does not change with the body, it remains behind. Just through this, we have it always before us and as we look at it, it mirrors towards us our experiences. The ego does not go with us on our earthly pilgrimage. The ego remains in the spiritual world."[1]

Dear friends, I personally knew of no greater anthroposophical nonsense than that which is often said about the ego. To the extent that people say: "My ego must be present, my ego must make decisions etc," these are perpetrations of nonsense that we make for the sake of nursing our beloved personalities. We usually speak about our ego with an unclear image. But Christmas extends to us an invitation to come a little nearer to its real existence.

The ego and what we believe the ego to be is related to the fruit of the Tree. The wonder of it is that through the way that Christmas has evolved in history we are guided to come a little nearer to this apple that hangs on the intertwined Tree of Knowledge and Life. When Christianity started to take hold of the civilization of Europe, Christmas was not cele-

---

1. Translation by Carlo Pietzner.

brated, at least not until the 4th century and even then in quite a different way from anything we usually imagine today. It was the coming of the Magi, the festival of Epiphany on the 6th of January, also the day the Baptism was celebrated. Only in 354 A.D. was the date for the birth-celebration of Christmas shifted to December 25th and it took at least 200 further years before Mass began to be celebrated at midnight at Christmas, thus marking Christmas in the sense of which we speak of it today.

What everybody remembered and which also remained longest as the bearer of the reality of the original impulse was, strangely enough, the Adam and Eve Day, the Paradise images, for which December 24th was the festival day. The major plays of Christianity which were soon acted in Europe were initially all Paradise plays. Only gradually were the Shepherds plays added to them. Later these were united with the Three Kings plays, as the celebrations fell ever more into decadence. These plays themselves went out of real usage, in that very serious way in which they had been handled for centuries, by about the middle of the 18th century. Then this tradition ceased altogether in Europe. It was then, that Schroer, for instance, but also Reinhold and others, started to pick up these plays in their original language. They had been written down in manuscript form from ancestor to child for centuries.

A few centuries before they fell into decay the situation in regard to these plays was still quite different. In the 15th—16th century they were by no means so holy, or so very serious. From about the 12th—13th century onwards, reaching into the 14th—15th centuries, these plays were developed by placing a crib or manger into the side chapels of the Cathedrals or churches. This was done by the clergy who were often not very learned people. They put the crib into the side chapels, with ox and ass and two puppets representing Mary and Joseph, and there was this crib for the child. It was difficult for the people to imagine what that meant. You must imagine that up to the 16th century very few people knew the Bible. It was one of the most important things for the clergy that those plays were played, that they provided an image. They wanted to do something for the people and their faith. So they put these cribs there and later on they began to play the relevant scenes— the clergy began to act a little bit so as to illustrate the meaning of these figures. They dressed up as Joseph and as Mary and then there was the crib, and they acted in Latin, too, and the people of course could not understand.

It seems to have been important for the clergy of these centuries to see to it that as few people as possible would understand what was said. So they did it all in Latin. These plays lasted for some time and the people could not really understand what it all was about. For there was a baby in a manger. They had never really seen a baby in a manger; it was also then not usual that a baby would lie in a manger. Nobody really knew why this baby was in a manger and the clergy, with very long faces, performed Mary and Joseph in Latin. But the people gradually wanted to be part of it. After all it had to do with God and His Son—so much they knew, of course, and they felt more in their deeply devotional concern. They insisted that at least part of these scenes should be played in the vernacular, that they should be translated. So some of these plays began to be translated in the 13th and 14th century. Deep down in some of the people there still lived the concept of the Sun-God from pagan times, the Son of God, who had come down to them in the dark of winter. They could not do much with this manger, it meant nothing to them at first. What this all-too human child in a manger had to do with these last remnants they still felt about the being of the Sun who had come to the earth—this had all to come together, had to be fused in their minds. But they wanted to be part of it. They wanted to experience something themselves.

What they then did was the following: they made a cradle instead of the manger and put the child into it, and now every one could understand that there was a new-born child laid into it and on top of it all they could now participate because they arranged it so that all the people that came into the church could go past this cradle and rock it. They started to participate by rocking the cradle and some of them joined in the chanting. They did not speak Latin. They could not join into the liturgy, but they could chant something when they rocked the cradle.

This was of course by no means necessarily a very holy affair. Rudolf Steiner describes it in a most lovely way. The people started to participate. They would come in and, even in a quite profane way, made a marvelous spectacle of it. Sometimes it went a little out of hand. They stamped into these chapels, they started to rock and to shout and to clap and to dance; some of them took their beer with them and it was by no means always holy. It was a festival to celebrate something in which everybody felt he was a part.

The wonderful development is that the thing itself began gradually to influence them. What had begun rather profanely, through the very holiness inherent in it, began to influence the people. They became more serious themselves. Gradually the scene itself began to transmit its holiness to the people at large. This is the way in which the influence of mysteries altogether work. They do not begin the other way round, with a long face, but they begin with the total involvement of the persons. This involvement is fostered by those who know in what way it should be guided and how it should take hold of the people. Gradually the thing by itself starts to transmit its reality—out of the image.

Thus it happened that the simplest of experiences—the folk festival way of celebrating the birth of a child—began to convey to all that it contained in itself something of the Christ; that, in fact, in each child's birth, if one becomes aware of it at Christmas time, the mystery of Christmas -the coming of the Christos into the human body—takes place. We are only at the very beginning of this mystery unfolding itself. But what begins to convey itself to all of us is the fact that the child, at the moment when he is born and as he takes from the spiritual world the forces of life and light into his body, works with the divine powers of innocence and purity. There are powers at work which are in fact of the same kind as those of the Christos. They work until the child becomes conscious of himself and says "I", then they stop. Then they become somewhat withdrawn and then only in an image can we communicate with Him.

The more we are able to turn toward these child forces consciously, the more are we able to revere the

manger in which, between ox and ass, this Christos
lies for us all.

At the same time one has to recognize that also
this knowledge is fed from the same sources out of
which all knowledge comes. The very knowledge can
at first spread like the incarnation of evil itself—over
everything that mankind does. Also the knowledge of
the ego grows from the sources from which evil itself
spreads, once the apple was bitten into. Even the un-
told disasters of our time have the same source: the
tree growing out of the mouth of Adam, out of the
tomb of Adam.

This tree contains—even though life is intertwined into it—all that can be imagined as evil. Yet we
are told that this tree is of such a wood that it has
served as the cross of mankind. It suggests that knowledge be gradually recognized to be the cross on
which the eternal child hangs. The child can be seen
related to this earth-cross.

There was a time called the 30-Years' War that
tried to cover this up. But there arose an image for
mankind, that was shown in many places in Europe,
in which a child was shown sleeping on the cross.

This image of the child, of the ego, sleeping on
the cross is where image *and* reality become one. This
child, this ego, the light of the Sun-man, sleeping,
laid upon the cross is at the same time the one which
I believe would perhaps enable us to find guidance in
our own attempts at celebrating Christmas today. It
will help us, I think, to feel image and reality come
closer to each other.

I would like to close with one further quotation by
Rudolf Steiner. It is a meditation which many of you
know. It sums up what I have been trying to describe.

This is a meditation which Rudolf Steiner gave expressly in order to strengthen the ego. It sums up the very core of the theme of image and reality, because it places it into this divine centre, into the crossing point of the two arms of the cross, the sleeping child of our ego.

> I look into darkness.
> In it arises light.
> Living light.
> Who is this light in the darkness?
> It is myself in my reality.
> This reality of my Ego
> does not enter into my earth existence.
> I am only an image of it.
> But I shall find it again
> when I—with good will for the spirit
> shall have passed through the portal of death.[1]

---

1. London, September 2, 1923—"*Man as a Picture of the Living Spirit*". Translated by Carlo Pietzner.

Christmas and Equilibrium

December 30, 1982, Beaver Run, PA

Dear friends,

I welcome you all tonight to Beaver Run as we admire the Christmas tree. It is a particularly beautiful tree, and it comes from Kimberton Hills.

It is a wonderful thing to turn toward Christmas. Our theme this year is the great being and power of Equilibrium. I think we have all asked ourselves, "Why Equilibrium at Christmas? Why BALANCE at Christmas?" It is not sufficiently known, but one can experience that Christmas—the Holy Nights, are a time to acquire balance. These are nights to attain to inner equilibrium so that it can be practiced throughout the year to come. The path through the Holy Nights is the way to acquire equilibrium which we need at the time when it becomes most difficult—at the other mid point of the year. It must be practiced deliberately, in May, June and July, when the world of nature tries to take us out of ourselves into the heights. To be prepared for this we need the balance that we can find at Christmas.

129

It is important to remember that true balance is not neutral but a high point of tension between extremes. It is a virtue, if you like, but it is also more than a virtue, it is a being that works in a virtue. Equilibrium is not particularly popular in our time. On the contrary, if something is good, let's have more of it. If one or the other thing pleases me, let me be pleased more! Our tendency is to get as much comfort and convenience as possible. And yet, this is a curious sickness of our time. Our time is meant to be a Michaelic time through us. We are meant to search for Michaelic qualities, and for balance. Equilibrium is the very kingdom of Michael. Michael is the guardian of equilibrium. If we turn at Christmas to balance, to equilibrium, we do so because we are led to relate to Michaelic impulses present at Christmas time. The german word for equilibrium is 'Gleichgewicht.' 'Gewicht' means weight, 'gleich' means equal and it gives us the association of equal weight. It is interesting to follow up variations of this and similar words, like balance. What stands behind these equal weights is the scale, the scale being the main activity, one might almost say the tool, one could also say the weapon—if that is properly understood, of Michael. The word equilibrium comes from 'aequus'—equal, and 'libra,' which is scale. Libra is the sign of the zodiac in which equilibrium is at home. It is the sign of Michael. The power of weight, the power of gravity and the power of levity and of light is associated with equilibrium and balance. Part of the meaning of equilibrium and balance is to overcome lukewarm neutrality and indecision. By then it has fallen into one of the two polarities. There is no assurance that a midpoint will be restored. Unless there is the expectation that it will be restored, the tension toward it, it does not exist. It does not exist without continuous re-creation. The moment it is allowed to lapse it is already part of the opposites between which it shall mediate. It is always, therefore, connected with the middle or midpoint. Christmas is the midpoint of the year. Christmas is the breathtaking midpoint of thirteen holy steps in the vast ongoing way through the seasons.

We have a similar correspondence that gives us much to think about. It is the East and the West and the absence of a true middle. There is a constant, almost instinctual need that always the one or the other of the two elements —East or West—have to add to its weight. As this happens, the other one must also add weight beyond any reason, beyond logic. The threat of potential catastrophe that arises is seemingly so large because of the loss of balance in our lesser activities. Loss of balance is of the same kind.

My question remains: "What is it that moves our hearts particularly at this time?" I do not know whether what I am going to say now will have a response in some of you. I know a number of people have felt like I during the last few days. I had to ask myself: "Who has stolen Christmas? Where has it been hidden? Where has it gone?" This question came to me as an old Camphiller who has been accustomed to celebrating Christmas for more than four decades mostly with a great intensity. One knows, as one has perhaps never known that the memory of Christmas will no longer suffice. The recollections and trappings have begun to confuse the reality of this festival to such an extent that they do not evoke by themselves the mood, the presence of this festival. And so one must ask: "Where do we find it?" It is to be found, perhaps, where it always has been found, only we must look differently. Where we must look to is toward the path leading us the way between two children, from one child to the other. It leads us from the child that is born and celebrated in the first Christmas night and who is described in the gospel of St. Luke, on through the Thirteen Holy Nights to that place where the second child is born, where the child of the St. Matthew's gospel, the Solomonic child appears. That is where we look for Christmas. It is on this way that we can acquire, in walking this path, balance and equilibrium.

The first child comes at night. It is Adam and Eve's night, when the birth of this first child is celebrated. The other one is the starbearer who had led the Kings to come. What stands behind these events? How can we see them? We have learned an unbelievable amount from Rudolf Steiner about these events. Without it we would be immeasurably poorer. We have learned through him to look at Christmas differently and we must learn constantly about this pathway between the two children. It leads from the birth of the child to the worship of the Three Kings, to the bringing of the three gifts which at the same time are indicative of another event: the event, *that* event of Christmas, which in the early times of Christianity was the real Christmas event, namely Epiphanias, the descent of the Christ into the body of Jesus at the Baptism of the Jordan on January sixth. It is this way which is beginning to open itself to a world event of great magnitude if we include all that takes place within the frame of the birth of the two children and the Baptism in the Jordan.

A few days ago I saw something which I had seen many times before and had wondered about. It was quite striking. It was the crib, the cradle. It is customary in this country to call this particular object a creche, and yet I feel slightly offended by the word. It is a beautiful French word and nothing shall be said against a French word, but it is almost representative, in the way it is being used, of something carved, pretty, often including shepherds *and* kings—all painted and lacquered. What I saw is something more beautiful, also more simple. It is better when we call it a crib. It is such a marvelous word with so many meanings. It is meant specifically to be a manger, a feeding trough for cattle or horses, and into it the infant Jesus was laid. It is a basket, originally, and has many associations. It is a lovely word, this crib, so is "manger." When I saw the object, I suddenly realized that I was confronted with a form which was an archetypal image. It was in this receptacle that a child was laid on behalf of the whole world, and rocked to and fro by Mary and Joseph. It helped to accustom this child, just out of the womb, to the equilibrium needed in this world. In the most gentle fashion, the crib provided the transition from the state in which the unborn human being has dwelled for so long, nine months, held from all sides, swimming in the fluid within the womb of the mother, so that when it is then placed within the conditions of the earth it may become accustomed to the change. It is released from the body and from the arms of the mother into this rocking rhythm. It is a first experience, a soothing, transient experience in which equilibrium plays a substantial part. It moved me, because I, suddenly, could feel myself—not into the Jesus child, this is an archetypal image—but into this cradle, as an object, which, when we attempt our descent into the flesh and are not yet able to stand in equilibrium, will hold us, in this gently rocking receptacle so that from the earth something answers the constant flow from heart to head, from head to heart. This gentle transition into space is a bridge which we ourselves have to build between two worlds. They would remain apart were it not for us human beings.

The sense of equilibrium is an important experience when one comes to the senses of the human being. One begins to understand how in every infant, (though there are some dim expressions of the sense of touch, of life, of self movement in relation to the life processes), it is through the sense of equilibrium that we first become aware of something *outside* ourselves. There is a mighty power which will make us fall over, pull us down if we do not regard it: gravity. It is on hand of equilibrium that the message comes to us: "You have come to a world of space within which gravity is at work."

It is a humble sense. We practice it in many different ways, as children do, when they stand on one leg, then on the other and balance with this, that or the other object. But we become conscious of it only when something is wrong with it. It must be present in all our creative activities which we wish to offer to the world if they shall be acceptable. This humble, mighty sense is the last bud on the enormous tree of incarnation which flowers when we are in the spiritual world. There it determines our relationship to the hierarchical world. It is in our relationship to Angels, Archangels and Archai, to Exusiai, Dynamis and Kyriotetes. This sense makes us aware whether we are in the presence, even if we cannot grasp it, of a Cherubim, a Seraphim, or a Throne. It is on hand of the sense of equilibrium now blossoming in the spiritual world that we may be aware of the higher beings in whose land we are. This mighty force is now condensed into the cradle, into this manger being rocked to and fro. On either side sit Mary and Joseph.

In this beautiful picture there are ox and ass. They are the first gentle reminder, the first warning presence of something which gradually, on its way to the earth, will unfold the greatest power with which equilibrium has to contend: Lucifer and Ahriman. There they sit as the first messengers in the world of space that is left and right. Adam and Eve stand behind this picture and sound the litany of sorrow: "What once upon a time was one, has become two."

We then go to the other end, where the kings appear who affirm the three great gifts not only to this child, but to every child by bringing myrrh, the bitterness of walking with one's destiny, frankincense as the cloud in which each human word will ascend to the Gods and finally gold, the light of thought. In this threefoldness there stands the gift and burden of becoming man—the descent of Christ into the human body. There is the gesture of the Baptist, who raises himself to the voice of the Father and the dove that hovers above the Being of the Christ, where we find the second spatial relation from below to upward, from upward to below. That is what happens toward the end of the Thirteen Holy Nights. We now begin to discover how the whole life of man depicted in this way is in need of acquiring balance. Balance is needed between the forces of growth and decay, between cleverness and lethargy, exuberance and apathy, of

light and darkness, of youth and old age, of round-
ness and crystal edges, of heat and cold, birth and
death. One can feel as if a Christmas guardian, Michael, would stand in front of this teaching of balance, as
a teaching of man's incarnation on his path of life between birth and the re-ascent to the spiritual world.

Rudolf Steiner gave a lecture on September 21,
1918 in Dornach dedicated to equilibrium. It was a
time full of despair, close to Michaelmas, and to the
end of the First World War and near the complete
collapse of so many things that still seemed to have a
human spark. He spoke then about equilibrium, in
particular about the third element, the most important one, which I already have mentioned tonight. It
is the one which has to do with the continuous battle
between overdevelopment and retardation, the battle
between Lucifer and Ahriman. We may ask: Where
has Christmas gone?—do we have to listen at Christmas to these dreadful things—evil powers, Lucifer
and Ahriman? We must. The mystery word of winter,
and with this of Christmas, is: Beware of Evil. To be
aware means to be consciously in balance.

I will quote from the lecture I have mentioned.
Rudolf Steiner says: "Ahriman would like to have laws
everywhere. Ahriman would like to write laws just like
this. It must be realized that human life in community is woven together from the hatred of Lucifer
against conformity on one side and out of Ahriman's
sympathy for conformity and regularity on the other.
Life cannot be understood unless it is understood in
this dualistic view. Ahriman loves all that belongs to
external form, all that can grow hard. The Luciferites
love every formlessness, all that dissolves and becomes fluid, movable. One must learn at the hand of

life to create equilibrium between the forces which want to harden and those which merely want to flow and become liquid"[1].

"At the hand of life," Rudolf Steiner says. At the hand of life! It is under the symbol of life, the tree of life, the Christmas tree, that we are to remember what is spoken in this lecture. Between the birth of the Nathanic Child and that of the holy steps of equilibrium, it helps us on the divine path of the human soul. It leads toward the becoming of man, Christ's becoming of man. At the midpoint between these events is New Year's Eve, is New Year's Day. In the manner of Janus this point turns to the past year and it also faces the future, the coming year. Looking back it says: "Yes, it has been." Looking forward it says: "What will it bring?" The past has been accomplished, however much sorrow it has brought and perhaps some shame—but it is memory. The future, not known to us, will harbor fear of the unknown: What will the next year bring?

There comes this moment, one of the most significant moments at the midpoint of winter, where we are called upon to develop balance between past and future. Everything unknown to us has a threatening aspect. The unknown heralds fear: the possibility of war, of tensions, of devastation—beyond our power of interference. It is there where we are challenged most seriously. Precisely there we must endeavor not to give in, neither to fear nor to apathy. There we need the Christmas message most urgently. To paraphrase, he says: "To the same extent

---

1. "Cosmic Prehistoric Ages of Mankind," 3 lectures, 20, 21, 22 September 1918, typescript. Translated by Mabel Coterell.

to which now and in the future you may be thrust below yourself by circumstances, to that extent you must rise spiritually above it"[1]. These are among the last words Rudolf Steiner wrote from his deathbed in his last letter to the members, when he spoke about Nature and Sub-Nature. We must learn to rise spiritually as high as materially we may sink or be thrust down.

This is the fruit of having learned during winter to be beware of evil: To wake up to evil as to something that is the same outside, in any form, as it is in me, learning to rise to the same extent as it wants to threaten and pull us down. It is the Christmas power of the Midnight Sun that can give us this possibility. It is the creative midpoint of Christmas, the Sun at Midnight.

Rudolf Steiner describes how we may build a place in our community efforts, through social art, where this Mid-Night Sun can rise. Rudolf Steiner describes how in the past the Oriental initiate, or adept, placed himself into the lotus position to reach up, away from the earth, to be out of the grasp of Ahriman. That is not what we can or should do. "But we can enter" as Steiner says, "through spiritual science into a land, which Ahriman cannot reach. Doing that we are enabled to meet Ahriman where we are meant to meet him, namely on our path on the earth"[2].

---

1. Letters to the Members "Das Goetheanum." ". . . Sub-nature must be grasped for what it is, and this can happen only if man rises at least as high above nature in a cosmic direction in pursuit of spiritual insight as he has descended with his technology to a sub-natural level . . ." March 1925, Dornach. Published: April 12, 1925, "From Nature to Sub-Nature." Translation by Marjorie Spock, St. George Publications, Spring Valley, New York, 1984.
2. Same as above (1), C. Pietzner's rendering in english.

Spiritual science, Anthroposophia, is present on one side of the cradle and she appears with gratitude also at the side of the Solomonic child when the three gifts of man are reaffirmed. Then, becoming rejuvenated in the spiritual world through what precedes the Baptism in the Jordan, she speaks to us today in the words that we, inasmuch as we regain forces of childhood, can hear her speak in us. So also do we feel her warnings, her help, her rocking, to obtain balance for our existence on earth.

Time Magazine cover, January 3, 1983

Christmas in our World

December 31, 1982, Beaver Run, PA

Dear Friends,

I have been asked to give a talk tonight—about "the world." I shall have to struggle through some darkness so that we may find something pertaining to the light of Christmas.

We use this word "the world" frequently, sometimes when it appears as a threat, and at other times as if it would be something desirable which we do not regard sufficiently. More often than not this is an over-simplification. It does not penetrate deeper than the first inch or two of a grey substance. However, time and again we have to consider our position in the world. We have to ask ourselves: What do we mean by this expression? What do we need to consider when we speak of the "world today"? Should I speak about "the" world? Is not what I mean as *my* world something quite different from *their* world, the world the media would have us believe exists around us as the main background of today?

Some of you may have seen the last issue of Time Magazine, one of the principal news magazines of the Western world. It is shattering to look at it. At this time of the year the cover picture of "Time" always shows the "Man of the Year", who was of greatest influence during the past year. Sometimes it was also a group of people. This year, for the first time, the Man of the Year is not a man but the "Machine of the Year", the computer. They gave a special commission to a famous contemporary sculptor, Segal, who exhibits in most modern museums. His specialty consists in the fact that he takes you and me, when we are sitting, perhaps well-dined, but always with tired abandon, casting us as we are, in our clothes, in plaster-of-paris or in papier-machè and then arranging us in a certain manner. Then he gives us a title. That is what he has done for the cover picture of the last number of "Time". There is a grey, plaster-of-paris, past-middle-age man sitting at a table in a totally empty room with a window that looks at nothing. There, too, is a woman, also in plaster-of-paris on the other side of the room. In front of each of them stands a computer on a small table, a small video screen, and on the video screen some graphs,—no Christmas tree, no creche or anything of that nature, but there are the two completely isolated plaster-of-paris-people around the "Machine of the Year." They represent total isolation, the garbage dump of communication between them, the end of communion between people. The picture is so gruesome, so heartbreaking, that I would ask everybody who thinks that he lives in our world to have a look at it.

It is altogether a remarkable number of "Time" because much of it is taken up with praise for the new revolution of the computer that will bring about a complete change in all our lives, I suspect even in the lives of our next incarnation, everywhere. It contains an update on the Book of Job. It is called: "The Updating of the Book of Jobs". That is Mr. Steven Jobs who is responsible for the Apple computer. He is just the very opposite of the Biblical Job. He is not a nice man, I think; he has never pleased God, he has only pleased himself. He is only 27 years of age and has managed to earn 210 million dollars in the last five years for himself. He almost made it to the cover page and he is a hero in our "world" of science.

If one looks at this double cover page of "Time" one can feel overcome by compassion and sorrow. We see two humanoid figures, an ox and ass in the shape of a man and a woman sitting around the new cradle, of the computer, in utter barrenness. It is true and real, I am sure, that they conceived this cover page and this article because the computer will do everything that it is prophesied to do. We too, of course, will use it—why not? It is intelligent to do so and we will have intelligent discussions on this topic, on how we must use the right thing at the right place. No doubt, it will save a lot of time-for what will remain a question.

This picture, I have no hesitation in saying, is one of the most powerful images Ahriman has painted until now. If you consider its implication you can say that these two people themselves represent the software which Ahriman has managed to produce out of us. This software sits there and manifests Ahriman, almost victorious already—Almost! For Ahriman is the master of the Almost.

So one must put the question: is *this* our world, your and my world, which is represented in all this? In this context one can now think of the first Christmas. One can recall how the events which took place at that time were recognized only by a handful of people, by a few individuals, not by "the world". After the birth, many years later, a great and true representative of the time, like Tacitus, the Roman writer, devotes exactly three lines to the insignificant sect which had given some trouble to the Roman Empire in Palestine. That is all that was officially recorded of Christianity by those who were "the world" at that time, who made history. We must not forget this and on the other hand try to realize that as a tiny handful of people we—I now mean us, and a few others—are confronted by certain things which we expect to happen. We expect the Second Coming of Christ, in the ether; we may assume that it has taken place for some people and we must expect that this will be possible in our world. This second birth has to do with a spiritual encounter and must also take place on earth, in our world. It is vital that it should take place on earth and one may ask what kind of world is needed for this to happen? Does it need special circumstances, could it not take place anywhere, in a factory, indeed in front of a video screen? Could it not take place, as it has perhaps happened, in solitary confinement in a political prison? Of course, it could take place anywhere. It does not require special circumstances of any kind. But it is not only the *event* itself, just as little as it was merely the event two thousand years ago, that took place. If it is not seen and understood it will pass by and have gone, even if it *has* taken place.

This gives us important and serious questions to carry. Are there places, at least a stable, that can give a space of recognition for this event? It is the *recognition* of the resurrection, and of the Second Coming that will matter. I want to be specific; how is it with regard to this with the "world of Camphill"?

It is very interesting to hear Camphill described by people, people who perhaps have had some inside experience of Camphill, even if only for a short time. We take it for granted that we understood and accepted from the beginning what, in shorthand, we call the mission of the handicapped. It means that one recognizes the total potential and humanness of a person, no matter how handicapped. It is the mission of the handicapped person to make that consistently visible, perhaps in the face of appalling difficulties. This assumption, this recognition, though not necessarily expressed with words I have just used, has spread all over the world, but from this recognition has not necessarily followed an action of Will. In Camphill we try not only to think it, although it is thrilling just as a thought. We began, almost from the outset, to build a world for the handicapped child—we did not know any better. The world of Camphill was gloriously infused by the power of the "Curative Course" by Rudolf Steiner, by Curative Education. We learned from the growing-up handicapped children not only to live *for* them, but to live *with* them. It made the founding of the first villages for adults possible and with it the development of specific social interaction started to be placed into the growing world of Camphill. It exists in variations all over the world.

Camphill began by taking will-consequences from an insight. Why do I stress this just this evening? That "World" which for a moment I see symbolized by the cover of Time magazine has been totally determined by the brilliance of our intellect. The absence of that

145

kind of brilliance and intellect is one of the significant characteristics of those who have taught us, the
handicapped person. In a lecture cycle which I hope
will, through the Section work of Curative Education
and Social Therapy, become in time the basic social
therapeutic lecture cycle[1], which Rudolf Steiner gave
in 1920, he speaks of the destiny of mankind during
the last three to four centuries through the prepon-
derance of intellectualism. He then continues to
speak about the forces that are being used in the attempt to bring about social forms in life and work, the
forces of the intellect, and says: "These forces are
working appropriately only then when they are destructive. Without these forces we could not think, we
could not develop our intellect; but we destroy the social order if it becomes permeated by the consequences of our intellectual activity"[2]. We destroy the
social order! Not only we, but thousands, millions of
people know it, feel it, but we can't strengthen this insight sufficiently so that people, at long last, wake up
out of the grip of Ahriman. One thinks about it and
then forgets again. This is the situation by which we
are surrounded and which can be contested through
Rudolf Steiner's insights. Rudolf Steiner continues:
"We need for our spiritual life, for our free spiritual
life, these forces of the intellect. We need them because that alone which the human intellect carries is
able to rise out of the chaos. But these same forces are
not suitable when they try to connect themselves with
social forms; this intellect becomes harmful, whilst it

1. Spiritual Science as a Foundation for Social Forms, (GA—199), Anthroposophic Press, 1986.
2. August 29, 1920, Dornach. Ibid—pg. 184, Lecturer's trans.

is useful within the confines of the free spiritual life. All that furthers the coming about of innovations," (computers and the like!), "what forms inspirited poems" (even those by Rilke), all that can arise out of chaos, out of the matured material of the human organism, it must never assume that it can give social impulses in relation to outer life. Everything must arise out of chaos which is to enhance spiritual life. Spiritual life must arise out of the chaotic ground of the individuality, of the human being"[1]. Here is truth; here is our legacy. Out of divine origin we bring with us from the holy fatherground the forces which now have become chaotic and they are useless for our social life. These forces are descending from the spiritual world into the earthly world and they have become chaotic forces. "We bring with us a decaying brain organism and from it, nevertheless, arises what constitutes the spiritual life, the cultural life. But it is at the opposite pole of the human organization where those forces must arise which can provide the fundaments for social ideals"[2]. The other pole is the metabolic limb-system; the legs, the arms. With and from these must arise the social forces. Rudolf Steiner says: "Let us understand that the whole human being must be taken into consideration. One believes to think only with the head. Man thinks, feels, wills not merely with his head, but with the whole organism. Arm and legs are of the same soul organism as the head"[3]. Giving room to thoughts which arise from our arms and legs is what we have to learn if the whole human being is

---

1. Ibid—pg. 184/5, Lecturer's trans.
2. Ibid—pg. 185, Lecturer's trans.
3. Ibid—pg. 185, Lecturer's trans.

to come into play for social interaction. "It is important to know that the single human being cannot do anything with numbers. Only Associations, groups of people can do something with numbers, because the groups can utilize their experiences and complement each other. However, such Associations will not achieve anything special unless they act out of directional forces, and what kind of directional forces are these? Those, which come out of imaginative knowledge arising from the science of initiation"[1].

These truths can remain for years in the realm of empty abstract words but when it goes beyond our superficial understanding one will be able to grasp the wisdom contained not only in these words but of every act of true work we have ever done with our hands and feet in the context of a Community. The moral strength of the directional forces to act faster than one can think with one's head alone is one of the great social powers available to the human being. Rudolf Steiner, after saying all this, then turns to a world audience: "This is a most important subject of which, in particular, the Anglo-Saxon, the American, world, must know because it is to be their responsibility to influence the power of the world. If they will not accept the spiritual responsibility for this task they will ruin the world"[2]. This is spoken to us, to your and my "world." It is with keen and almost ruthless eyes that we must time and again test the texture of our own world of Camphill. We must insist on those things which are valid because they relate to a space of understanding for important events to take

1. Ibid—pg. 189, Lecturer's trans.
2. Ibid—pg. 190, Lecturer's trans.

place in individuals but which do not arise from the chaotic forces of the intellect.

When we speak about the opposites of thinking and willing, the head and the metabolic system, we usually think that *we* are the only ones to think. That is a tragedy which limits our thoughts about thinking.

I can only think because I, myself, have been thought by a spiritual being. Spiritual beings who belong to our world and who are anxious that we should live in a cosmos to which we belong, which is appropriate for us and our mission, continually think and will and in doing so, since the beginning of time, create. There are other beings who are not born into a physical body, but act into the etheric and astral fashioned into physical matter. They work into earth, air, water, fire, into the rhythms of day and night and into the movements of the planets and of the earth. These are the constantly creative elementary beings. We are meant to live in awareness of them, particularly at Christmastime, because they have one peculiar characteristic in common, in that they cannot experience a small child. Childhood in the earthly cosmos would have to be translated for them through man's existence and being.

For each age group there are different experiences, particularly for those between 42-49 years of age, which has the most difficult relationship between man and these elementary beings. These beings either help us or make difficulties for us. Sometimes they make it difficult because they want to, at other times because we carry them unknowingly like millstones around our neck.

Rudolf Steiner describes four ways, in particular, in which that can be felt. The first is a feeling of emptiness concerning nature over which one has seemingly no control; a certain anxiety even, for feeling unrelated, for having no experiences of nature. The second is a feeling of inertia, paralysis of the will, resistance against cognitive activity. The third has to do with a mostly unconscious feeling of displeasure, never allowing one to be truly joyful. The fourth is related to difficulties with religious experiences as the direct outcome of our blindness and unrelatedness to elementary beings.

You might say: "What can we do?" "Why do we have it so difficult?" Now we must redeem these beings, add still another exercise, perhaps? We should not overlook that these feelings are the very stuff of the double, our own double, our shadow being. Our whole earthly existence over many incarnations is meant to redeem that double. It is made of our unfulfilled relationships to the elementary beings.

How has it come so far, prepared for many years, that something which many of us have experienced— that Christmas is like a hallowed space, surrounded by ox and ass—has now begun to become hidden from us by certain elementary beings who snatch it away here and there, not allowing us to have that old Christmas experience? Behind all this lies something which we should not cover up with tinsel to make it look a little better. We should look it straight into the eye. If one does this one can recognize a tremendous promise, a message, that is possible to fulfill if we are willing to empty ourselves and no longer pretend or hide behind masks. In this promise there works, unknown to us, the Second Coming of the Christ which also works into the elemental world. Rudolf Steiner expresses it like this: "At the turning point of the 20th century there will be born a new kingdom of nature beings. Like a spiritual fountain it will arise out of nature and become visible and capable of being experienced by man"[1]. Christ's appearance in the etheric world will bring this about. Rudolf Steiner continues: "As the ether body will develop, aided by the Autumn impressions which weave into man's inner organization, human beings will perceive the etheric Christ. What was the reason of the birth of the physical Christ? It happened so that the human being could advance himself in his evolution and thereby become able gradually to perceive Christ in the etheric realm"[2].

The *first* Christmas then is the reason to give the possibility for the Second Coming. This is the promise hidden in our struggles.

It is important to acknowledge to ourselves that we do allow our social life to be influenced by the intellect. Instead of permitting a moral action to work through our limbs, over and over again, by intellectually pondering and charting the way, we fail to perceive behind every simple or complex material object the constant struggle and interweaving of the elemental world, a world which is being supplemented, if not replaced by, a new etheric kingdom of beings. We allow our materialistic insights to deal almost exclusively with our everyday existence, be it in our houses, our work or with any object we are entrusted with. This is what we can experience at times as "our world" situation. It is just in this our world where we

---

1. September 19, 1911, Locarno—*The Christ Impulse in Historical Development.* Lecture II "Esoteric Christianity and the Mission of Christian Rosenkreutz," 2nd revised edition 1984. R. Steiner Press, London.
2. Ibid. pg. 29/30

have a chance to be the molders and the conductors of our lives and to prepare a consciousness for the coming of Christ in the world of the ether.

LECTURE TEN

The Light of the Fourth King
A Saint Paul's Address

January 26, 1986, Camphill Village, Copake, NY

Good evening dear friends:

I am grateful that we can be together for this St. Paul's festival, if it can be called that. It is a strange and amazing, never ending story, full of riddles. And although what this event may have historically looked like has been engraved in our minds, these are only approximations of the extraordinary thing which happened outside Damascus to a man known for his zeal and his fury, whose name was Saul. He was on his way to Damascus, and it is not certain from the several descriptions in the Bible whether it was through the flashing light that was suddenly all around him that he was blinded, and which the others who were with him also experienced, or whether it was something he *heard* that made him unable to find his way as a seeing person. This and many other things belong to the riddle of how Saul became Paul.

If any of us would walk to a place full of expectations, and what happens on the way is able to change us so profoundly that we become a different person throughout, and some other name would be given to us, we would be called anew to a life that we had not been able to imagine before. This is related to a story which I cannot tell tonight. It is the wonderful story of Christian Rosenkreutz, who calls someone before he falls down a mountainside or crosses a street, and calls him by his name. From that moment on (that person's name may remain the same) he is changed. His life is given to him anew and he is to offer it in the service of those who gave it to him. Paul has been described as an artist and a writer; but he was more than that. He was a philosopher, an orator, a brilliant speaker, a small man burning himself up with the fire of his conviction. There is still more which, as yet, has not been sufficiently acknowledged; that he became the creator of a kingdom, a kingdom of Christendom. He did not create Christianity, but he, by his zealous work and unceasing labor on his journeys all over the world, embracing the Mediterranean landscape right up to Rome, began to create a kingdom of which he himself, even to this day and by the power of his word, is the acknowledged king.

Paul became a king. He became a king without outer trappings. And unbeknownst by the other kingdoms of the world he walked the earth. I pondered about St. Paul this year as I have done for many years, and what this might mean to us as a group. What does it mean that, recurring every year, there is the day when we turn to this event of Saul becoming Paul, the founder of Christendom?

I thought of the pictures that exist in many different variations all over the world of another person, another great, great person who might be called the forerunner of the king. It is John the Baptist, who with his strange kind of garment, with his simple life in the desert, calling out with his mighty voice, perhaps a mightier voice than that of St. Paul, predicted the coming of Christianity, the coming of the Messiah. If one thinks about it, if one listens to his speech, grandiose though his words are, telling the sons of Abraham what they have to do, he does not hide from them what they have to do in order to become members of the coming kingdom. If one listens to this for a while, one can have the feeling that he was a shepherd king. Despite his mighty call upon people, he did it with the attitude, the humility and the care of a shepherd. And then, as you know, we come to Christmas and there came three kings, the three Magi. They came from very far away, from very different places.

The one thing that united them with each step since they started from their own land toward their common goal, apart from their expectation of the Messiah and the prophesy of finding the child that would become the Messiah, was a star. The star, a light, if you like, which shines a long, long time and follows its course over the enormous vault of heaven, guided the Three Kings. One king was garmented in red, the second in blue, the third one in green. They wore these garments because the red one had the color of gold, of wisdom. The blue had its symbol in silver and speaks of the reflection of divine love in the human heart. Green is copper, and works deeply into the human being who is at work upon the earth.

There is a persistent story. There are actually a number of different stories, some of them are very well known, others are less well known. Some of them are written with deep inner devotion, some of them cynically, but there is the persistent story of a Fourth King. There was a king on a journey who for various reasons was not present at the time when the other three united and met with one another. The fourth seemed to stay behind or in some way or other was so urgently needed by events that happened to people around him that time and again he missed his way. He was delayed in trying to attend and care and look after all the people that needed him.

This king, if he is pictured well, is one who came with the pure color of kingdomhood. He came with the color that previously only kings and priest-kings were permitted to wear, which has been quite forgotten by Anthroposophists, namely purple. That was the color which only the highest leaders were permitted to wear. It was to express the inherent ability to rule, to lead, but not in mighty outward ceremony, but with humble respect for the needs of the people. And this purple, as I shall explain a little later, is the symbol of life. Life is, so to speak, represented by the color purple.

What this purple king carried as a gift was *true thought.* The gift of the fourth king which he has come to offer is *true thinking.* This king was also the carrier of thought. He was the carrier of thought that thinks of itself, not only of things. That is already difficult to understand properly: *to think about thinking and not about that which is thought of.*

It is this kind of thinking which Rudolf Steiner described early on when he wrote *Philosophy of Spiritual*

Activity pointing to it as the new thinking; that it be exercised in peace and quiet. This purple king is truly not only the carrier of thought but also the carrier of light. Yesterday we spoke about the comets, how the light carriers of the crystals are pressed together in these formations with which the comets circle throughout space. Warmth, inner warmth, outer warmth, warmth altogether can ray into three directions of space. When we speak of light we must speak of a fourth dimension, inwardness. Light must be able to expand into a fourth dimension, the inward one.

Why is it always said of St. Paul that he was born before his time? There must be some relation to this in that he could bear something of this tremendous inner upheaval that others were not yet able to bear; something which was not reflected in earthly life and physical phenomena but in inwardness.

The Christ who is seen as if he would be in the physical as a person, as a figure is, nevertheless, totally inward, inwardly shining, inwardly radiating. This expectation of what gradually begins to appear among mankind, sometimes in single people here and there, is also the most difficult one, but it has to be mentioned. It is something which seems totally contradictory and yet can be a fact for anybody.

One cannot *think* light. One can only *see* what light brings about if it falls on an object. It is utterly impossible to see light per se. All that we see is called forth by light, but light *itself* is not visible. For instance, a candle is just dark matter and substance which is lit up by a light which we cannot see. Different colors, different planes, the wick within the wax, all this contributes to the "candle light" as you put a match to it; you set it alight (which you can see) but you cannot see the light itself. It is not directly visible, but is expressed through the physical properties of the candle. This is the same as what happened to Paul. If we were to be suddenly "illumined" by light itself, we would be overcome by the reality of light and be blinded by the light that shines upon the earth. It is an extremely fascinating thing to try and weigh up certain things which belong to this difficult and wonderful subject. It is interesting to reflect upon the following small paragraph—it is part of a conversation which Rudolf Steiner had with somebody else about light where he says the following: Electricity is light in a submaterial condition[1]. Light pressed together can engender the experience of the inner etheric Christ as something that comes to expression as the language of a natural law. Within our own being, yours and mine, there is something which is gradually changing our whole organism in its entirety so that it becomes transparent for the experience of the etheric Christ as an event of natural law. That is the one stream, the microcosmic inner human stream which must be taken into consideration. It is active particularly when we sleep, enters the region of our heart, and streams up to our brain.

There is yet another stream, an outer one, which is also working with the force of a natural law. It has to do with the reality of the Mystery of Golgotha. Two thousand years ago the blood of Christ entered the earth in such a way becoming consecrated to the earth that it began to unite with the earth and gradu-

---

1. Rudolf Steiner writes about this in his letters to the members March 1924, contained in "The Michael Mystery" (From Nature to Sub Nature, April 12, 1925). St. George Publications, Marjorie Spock Translation, 1984, p. 173. German edition: Leading Thoughts, #183-185.

ally, very gradually works through the earth to reach
the human being. That is why it appears as a natural
event in which everyone is able to participate. One
does not necessarily have to know anything at all
about it; to have devotion is necessary. While that is
so, the meeting of the inner stream, the microcosmic
one, with the one that develops like a natural law, the
macrocosmic stream, is dependent on us. If we cannot unite these two streams, if we do not bother about
them, try to understand and touch something of
them, we can neither enter into the sphere in which
light can be seen, nor can we participate in the beholding of the sheaths of the being of Christ in the
ether realm.

And so one wonders how that was. Paul, still Saul,
intent upon what he thought to be a righteous path,
carrying the letters of the high priests on the way to
Damascus in order to get hold of all those who pro-
claimed stupid nonsense about the Messiah, experiences sudden flashes around him and a voice speaks
to him. The others can hear but not see where it
comes from. And He told: "The one whom you perse-
cute is the Messiah."

That is the understanding of which I am speaking. This is what people need to know if they want to
grow inwardly: that they do not only have an experience, but that experience gradually becomes understood in its context, a new kind of light-permeated
knowledge which, mostly, we are too lazy and undisci-
plined to pursue. And then it happens: he fell to the
ground, the light flashing around him and then he
was up but could not go about as usual because he was
blind to the earth. He had begun to see what others
could not see, but at the same moment he had begun

to be blind to the light of the earth. It is a strange and amazing thing. It is a condition where without losing consciousness, one is able to see in a realm where Christ now is in the condition of clairvoyance. It is "clear seeing," clair-voyance. It is the ability to move according to the inner light.

Let us look at it once more. There are the three kings whose festival actually does not end until we have reached the festival of the Fourth King. If all had participated in this process, we would understand why it is said of Paul that he was born before his time. He could do all this long before any one of us, before others, could develop the same activity. The processes that have been described in their more external aspect can also be perceived in man through clairvoyance. When a man stands in front of us today in his waking stage and we observe him with the eye of clairvoyance, certain rays of light are seen streaming continuously from the heart toward the head. Within the head, these rays play around the organ known in anatomy as the pineal gland. These streamings arise because human blood, physical substance, is perpetually dissolving itself into etheric substance. A continual transformation of the blood in the region of the heart into this delicate etheric substance which streams upward toward the head and shimmers around the pineal gland takes place. This process of the relation of the blood to the pineal gland can be perceived in the human being all the time during his waking life. The occult observer is able to see a continuous streaming from outside into the brain and also in the reverse direction from the brain to the heart. These streams, which in sleeping man come from the outside, from the cosmic space of the macrocosm and slowly into the inner constitution of the physical body and the etheric body which is lying in bed, reveal something very remarkable to the investigator.

The rays vary greatly in different individuals. Sleeping human beings differ drastically from one another. If those who are a little vain only knew how badly they betray themselves to occult observation when they fall asleep during public gatherings, they would try their level best not to let that happen! In the case of a man who has only a slight inclination towards moral principles the rays gleaming into him are a brownish red. In a man of high moral ideas the rays are light violet in color. At the moment of waking or going into sleep, a kind of struggle takes place in the region of the pineal gland between what streams down from above and what reaches upwards from below. When a man is awake, the intellectual element streams upwards from below in the form of light and what is of a moral nature streams down from above. At the moment of waking or going into sleep these two currents meet and in the man of low morality a violent struggle between the two streams takes place in the region of the pineal gland. In the man of high morality there is around this gland a little seed of light. Moral nobility is revealed when a calm glow around the pineal gland is dispersed. In this way a man's moral disposition is reflected and this calm glow of light often extends as far as the heart. The streams therefore can be perceived in man. The one, macrocosmic, the other microcosmic.

Properly seen, *the activity of Paul relates to the building of the purple kingdom.* This is the kingdom of the heart. Properly understood the kingdom of Christendom is meant to become the kingdom of the heart. Its king is a purple king. The purple king was not like other kings of his time who appeared in mighty shining armor, big sword and shield with crown and scepter, he was all man—Paul. He took into himself all that which must be taken into man, into his inwardness, into the fourth dimension, to allow light to be sensed with love.

If you want to be a painter, and depict persons, you take colors and try to mix them, basically using red and blue. You mix these together, you will get different kinds of violet and purple. It is the same purple that only kings were permitted to wear. You can just use purple, you can, of course, use anything today; you can do what you please. When you use purple you must choose very carefully where you put it, otherwise you put it into prison because purple wants to radiate. Inwardly, purple comes about through the fact that red and darkness of blue are mixed together very quickly, over white. The color that appears is not the dark purple of the mantle of kings, but is the color of the human spectrum. It is the incarnate, the color that the image of man in time to come will wear, because there is no race today, black, brown, white or any other that wears this color. For this color is meant to be the inward purple which Paul was . . . and carried.

Finally, let me say this: to carry the light of the inner man was the task of Paul, as king, as the bearer of the inner purple, of the incarnate. Become aware of color! Re-enter the kingdom of purple, the kingdom of which Paul was the first king!

LECTURES ELEVEN & TWELVE

Sacrifice in Relation to
Palm Sunday and Easter Sunday

Palm Sunday, April 15 &
Easter Sunday, April 22, 1984, Camphill Village, Copake, NY

Palm Sunday, April 15, 1984

Dear Friends,

Palm Sunday with its might, its grace and wonder, is meant to be the beginning of our Easter celebration. We have participated many times in the celebration of Palm Sunday. It is always different and yet it is always the same, always inexhaustible.

This year we hope to link our efforts to these remarkable words which Rudolf Steiner spoke, when he made us aware that from our time onwards we will begin to see the Christ, not in the physical world, but in his etheric appearance. This important message, this revelation, is perhaps the foremost reason for the existence of Anthroposophy. There is much else that would contribute to our understanding toward this fact of the reappearance of the Christ in the etheric world. One motive which accompanies many of the lectures Rudolf Steiner gives on the subject and which has to be assimilated is the being of Abraham. We are living in the time which dates 2000 years, approximately, since the event on Golgotha, and 2000 years before that Abraham lived. When we allow ourselves to dwell upon the many legends and stories which tell us about Abraham it is important to grasp why we may wake up to something related to Abraham.

I would like to recall something I saw this morning. There were a few fleeting moments when it was a little milder and when the clouds opened, the sun shone through the clouds. It had something special to it, a certain glitter which appeared on the pond. It lit up the wet roads as if reflecting ice or snow with a fine rain in between. The birds, which so often like to sit close to the branches of a tree or bush, did not mind. Not only were they flitting to and fro, but they seemed to present themselves to this rain. The robins were hopping on the lawn as if it was sunshine—which, indeed, it was, albeit for a few moments. One could see once again, even if only for a moment, that the yearly conquest of the sun had started in earnest. In this short, incredibly harmonious moment Palm Sunday had appeared! The sun had entered its earthly inheritance! It had entered a place, as it will have done in many other places too, which, inasmuch as these places are habitations of man, however silently and unmentioned, may always be called Jerusalem. There is always "Jerusalem" where men live in peace and there is no "Jerusalem" where men do not live in peace. Into this the sun has come. One may say that it was not only the light of the sun making this moment so overwhelmingly beautiful. It was a presence as it can be experienced now and then at Eastertime. A presence of beings. A presence of divine beings. It was as if before our beholding souls there was displayed what sacrifice is, with such total abandon and utter giving as perhaps no other thing, creature, or being is more capable of than the sun itself. It was a moment of giving away substance in beauty. It takes some effort to convey that.

The verse of the soul calendar for this week contains the wonderful line: ". . . . and beauty wells from outer width of space"[1]. Living with this ever new, never-to-be-exhausted Palm Sunday Word for a long time: when beauty wells forth, streams forth, wells out of the width of space, one can have an inkling that it does not mean that our eyes see something at that specific point or place. It is as if an important substance is given out of the width of heaven, and from the reaches of the cosmos like an inexhaustible well which springs forth through the power of Palm Sunday; the well of beauty! This is echoed in the calendar of the soul verse of Easter Sunday, next week, which begins: "When out of width of worlds the Sun speaks to the human sense and joy from depth of soul in vision joins with light . . . "[2].

Not often do these words occur in the Calendar of the Soul; *beauty* and *joy*. Beauty as a source of existence is linked through this week with joy as a substance which out of man's soul tries to answer the message of the light. The sun speaks to the human

---

1. "The Calendar of the Soul" by Rudolf Steiner; verse 52 Palm Sunday. Anthroposophic Press, U.S.A., 1974.
2. "The Calendar of the Soul" by Rudolf Steiner; verse 1, Easter. Anthroposophic Press, U.S.A., 1974.

sense, and joy from depth of soul . . . Joy from out of the depth of soul! It does not mean to be in a good mood, as something natural and a matter of course. It is a fruit of Easter. It is possible that just at Easter life with all its troubles and great and small difficulties, with its appreciations and satisfactions, yes, and also with its joys, can begin to induce not only words of conversation with one another but words which gradually reach out and speak with the Gods.

For this we need to understand that our religious life is one that the Gods expect us to feel the whole week through, not only on Sunday morning. For religion is as much in goodness, as it is in beauty, as it is in truth. To develop this belongs to the true inheritance of man which must not be made small through our neglect of conversation. If this becomes something we can gradually touch upon by the way we conduct our life during Passion Week, then not only *we* may learn to feel here and there that our words reach out to the Gods, but the *Gods* may perhaps speak again to us. Not only in our prayer do we learn to speak to the Gods, but in our inner pictures, through our offering of thoughts.

Rudolf Steiner speaks about this in a wonderful passage. He says: "Let us try to imagine as clearly as possible that we look at a rose. We look at it in such a way as if we would see it for the first time and we are overcome by its beauty"[1]. Relating this to what I have said before we could say that out of the well of beauty would flow this awe; like the religious experience of the beauty of the rose. Rudolf Steiner continues: "If

---

1. "The Evolution from the Standpoint of Reality and Truth", Lecture II, 11/7/1911. pg. 27. Rudolf Steiner Publications, London, 1954.

we feel this beauty with a certain amount of bliss we then put ourselves into the position of beings who watch a sacrifice taking place. We watch how in this outpouring of beauty something is offered up which spiritual beings, watching a sacrifice, experience with such great echoing response of joy and activity, that they wish to give themselves away, all they have, and pour it as their own virtue, as an offering, into the world. We approximate the intense spiritual beholding which the spirits of wisdom, the Kyriotetes, enact when they watch the sacrifice of higher beings"[1]. This we approximate when, looking at the rose, we are overcome by bliss at the outpouring of its beauty. This is what I meant when I described to you this morning's moment. It was so beautifully pure that just watching it was as if one would be present at a sacrifice pouring itself out and the sun taking hold of its human heritage. The wish to give away began to stir within the onlookers.

This is a kind of overture to the great wonder and riddle of sacrifice, what it may be, where it comes from and how we human beings are meant to partake. We have turned to Abraham in the wider context of the lectures on the theme of the reappearance of Christ in the etheric world and we turn to him in particular because of this extraordinary story of Abraham's willingness to sacrifice his own son Isaac.

It is said that Abraham's father, Terah, was a kind of leader of soldiers, a general, under a great but mysterious king in Babylon. This king was more than a king, who still had the mythological being not fully man, a giant like Gilgamesh. His name was Nimrod,

---

1. Ibid. Pg. 27. (Carlo's own rendering of English translation.)

which means someone who is in revolt, who lifts himself and all he does up to greater heights. He therefore also becomes the builder of the Tower of Babel. At the time when this general was expecting a child, Nimrod had a dream. In this dream he was told that the child to be born would dethrone many kings and rulers, and Nimrod became afraid. He had never been afraid before. As the legend tells, Nimrod ordered the child to be killed. It is also said of him in many legends that he caused the death of many children and their mothers, even more than died through Herod. One legend says that 70,000 mothers were killed. It seems with their mothers also the children were obliterated. But Terah had hidden his child, the mother and the child. He had hidden his wife and the child, which was to be Abraham, in a deep cave. It was through this ruse guided by the Gods that the child Abraham was spared. There are different accounts of how long he lived in that cave. The important point is that for the first three years of his life this child had to live alone in the cave. His mother could not be with him and so God made it that this child could feed himself by sucking the fingers of his own right hand. He could live and become what he did by performing this extraordinary act of sucking milk from his own finger. It is a strange thing and everybody today is entitled to wrinkle his forehead in disbelief. But I believe it *is* an amazing thing. It is one of the wonders of the world to see a mother suckling her child. It is already apparent, although quite differently so, when one sees the feeding of piglets or of a calf, or any other creature, sucking from its mother. It is most deeply moving with a mother and her child because it is through the mother's breast that the child is led from the wide cosmos into earthly existence. It is included in the world. The mother offers herself to convey to this little child through her milk, through her being—the birthright of this child upon earth. In some of the tribes of the past a child that had not been suckled by the mother was not yet considered to be born. It was not yet considered to be living on earth. Indeed, if the child had a defect it could be put away and the soul was told to try again, because as yet the child had not been born. The child was a citizen of the earth from the moment it received the milk of the mother. Then the whole tribe would stand around and protect it. Now we are to imagine that this was not so with Abraham. According to the legend he was suckling himself. By the grace of God he was made to develop and to grow on this earth by doing something completely singular. He, who knows the circle of the wide world, he becomes a circle of his own by sucking his own finger. This is described in a remarkable way at a much later part of this legend; he was forty-eight years old at that time and was put into prison by Nimrod. He was in danger of being killed and his father, Terah, and others with him prayed to God for the rescue of Abraham. And God answered: "I am the single One and Abraham is *my* single One. Thus it behooves the single One to rescue the other single One." So unique was Abraham that he was able to draw his own nourishment out of himself.

It is a significant thing to suck one's thumb. If children do that for too long it is important to take notice. It is as if they need to become aware of themselves by the wrong means. There is a painting of the creation of Adam by God as painted by Michelangelo.

It is one of the great mythological pictures of the human soul for all times. Here you see the most magical of all moments taking place when from the hand of God power goes over into the hand of Adam. Nourishment of the most intimate kind can happen since the hand has come into touch with the divinity, the divine being who creates his own single, unique One. All this has to do with the remarkable being of Abraham.

Abraham was the first one who could live entirely in himself because he could picture in himself and through the power of his thought the Godhead, the divine being. Through him all those who would follow, his sons, his grandsons and further offspring would learn in time by the hereditary stream of blood, to do the same: to become inwardly able to be entirely their own selves and to think God. It makes the question of Abraham's sacrifice so deeply puzzling. How could it be that this precious being, the singular One, to be developed in Abraham, and to be so developed that this singularity could gradually be passed on to further generations—that this should suddenly be interrupted, undone! How could it even be thought of that this could be made *not* to work through the death of Isaac, who was meant to be the one to hand over these new gifts and talents through his children and grandchildren into the Jewish tribe. This must stand before us as a question.

What does it mean to offer a sacrifice? What stands behind the meaning which has to do with—making whole-holy—? What does it mean to be singled out by either having a certain gift or a special possession and then to be asked to give it away? What stands behind such a gesture? Whereto does it flow?

We can concentrate upon this question within the range of our own experience. We can read or hear about a person: what goes on in the soul if one offers up something, if a sacrifice is made? It is a tremendous thing to be attained and has played a great role in the building up of Camphill. Without the continuous weaving of sacrifices there would be nothing of Camphill in this country.

The phrase is often used fairly quickly: "I sacrifice my free time." It is, of course, an important thing to give it away if one feels one has earned a free afternoon. Many have done it and, we hope, will do it in the future. It matters that one does it out of oneself, doing it freely. But there are bigger things. There is a word in the life of Camphill which created more warmth and caused more struggle than any other word. It says: "To sacrifice one's own volition in the service of higher aims." One can say it in different ways to make it more understandable, but this is what it amounts to. Here we come to one of the most important aspects which touches upon the life or death of people's relationship with one another.

What is it now that weaves through our considerations? The most breathtaking thing is hardly ever thought about although it is its most significant ingredient, important with regard to any sacrifice. It is even greater than the sacrifice itself: whether or not a sacrifice will be accepted. If a sacrifice is to be offered, gradually becoming a longing in the human soul to be given away, it is of the greatest imaginable power if such an effort is being refused. Such refusal to accept a sacrifice is by no means only a negative thing. It does not have necessarily negative consequences. We must recall that this whole complex stands at the beginning of man's history, where we find the sacrifices offered by Cain and Abel. We have forever before our souls how one of these sacrifices was acceptable to the gods, Abel's and—however beautiful and carefully prepared—Cain's sacrifice was not. It was refused.

Therefore the question which runs together with the meaning of sacrifice has to do with the possibility that a sacrifice will be refused. We have to consider when we turn to Abraham that he was prepared to sacrifice Isaac, his son, and this sacrifice was renounced. Instead of Isaac a young lamb, a ram was found caught in a tree and sacrificed.

This brings us to the greatest of all sacrifices, to Easter itself, the sacrifice of the Being of Christ. Thus there arises, and is continuously at work in us throughout this Passion Week, the question: how is the sacrifice on Good Friday made acceptable when on Easter Sunday the rising from death occurs for all men?

This may lead us into this Holy Week and toward Easter Sunday.

Easter Sunday, April 22, 1984

Dear Friends,

Let us recall some of the events during the days of Holy Week.

On Monday, under the sign of sun and moon, we heard the parable of the fig tree. On Tuesday, in a noble and solemn way, the gift of mars spoke in its misuse and in its tender use. On Wednesday we heard and saw the story of Tobit who became blind and Tobias who went out to heal his father with the help of Raphael. On Thursday we attempted to live in the celebration of the sevenfold candlestick of Melchizedek. Those were the subjects of this week. On Friday, we saw the play of the union of human suffering which we follow, on our way always, whoever we are. Then, on Saturday, we met the threefold dialogue which takes place within each human being while, within the silence of the tomb, the resurrection is being prepared. Today we experienced the culmination, particularly also of this wonderful music which moved through these days, "The Seven Days of Holy Week," a traditional text with music composed by Christof Andreas Lindenberg and the holy web of the Services holding everything together. It lead us in particular from the night of Good Friday to the glorious celebration this morning in the light of Easter Sunday when its warmth mingled with joy which ought to live in the human soul at this occasion.

A cycle of lectures by Rudolf Steiner aids the understanding of sacrifice. One might say that it could be called a guide for understanding sacrifice. Five lectures, given in Berlin between October 31—December 5, 1911 are a kind of anatomy of sacrifice and its role in evolution and in man's soul. *"Evolution from the Standpoint of Reality and Truth"* is the title. These lectures contain a wonderful description and call on the resources of the world and of man in relation to sacrifice. These lectures can lead us to understand how everything in evolution, whether cosmic or human, is founded on sacrifice and why that is so. It is described how the planetary evolutions are based on sacrifice and the hierarchical evolution of the beings of the Gods, and also that of man. Warmth is the substance and the source of all sacrifice. It will give us a feeling of the landscape which we are about to enter if I read a few lines from this lecture cycle. "Everywhere, where there is warmth we have in truth sacrifice, an offering up"[1]. A little later Steiner says: "Conditions of warmth are the outer, the physical, expressions of sacrifice." And then follows a sentence we would do well to ponder, "No one can know what warmth is who is not in a position to form a concept of what it means to surrender, to be capable of offering what one possesses or is—yet, not only capable of surrendering to sacrifice what one *has* but what oneself *is*"[2].

In exalted and yet clear and simple words sacrifice is spoken of and our understanding might be immensely enhanced if we could translate the meaning of the inner action, the inner experience of this action by living for a while with these words.

I will continue about one particular aspect related to our theme. It is a social aspect. We spoke about

---

1. 5 Lecture II, Pg. 27. Anthroposophical Publication, Co., London, no date for publication.
2. Ibid. Lecture III, Pg. 37 (Carlo's rendering of English translation).

Abraham and came to this all important moment in Abraham's life when he has to fulfill, out of his devotion for the Godhead, the call that had told him to sacrifice his son Isaac. Perhaps we do not sufficiently imagine how at that time and also nearer to our time, sacrifice was an ongoing event, continuous, without which life would not have been able to exist. This holds good not only for one but for nearly all known people who lived on earth. It was a different kind of sacrifice though, than we are accustomed to today. If you read *Homer*, the *Iliad* or the *Odyssey*, or Vergil's *Aeneid*, the journeys of Aeneas from Troy, you will find that on every step which is being taken sacrifices are being offered. These may be a clutch of turtle doves, it may be a heifer, it may be three black sheep, a bull or a lamb. Always there are offerings, specific ones for specific gods and always of the most precious kind which the king, the farmer, the simple traveler has to offer from his possessions. But it is continuous, even if it is only a cup of wine or oil poured as a libation over the altar or lit. Every step took place in awareness of the gods, in awareness of not being alone, never being on one's own, within one's responsibility for making decisions. One knew that one's every action would affect the world of the gods.

Their advice inside the boundaries of necessity and freedom was sought for and attempted to be lived. Many practices of these sacrifices became decadent and took on a powerful life of their own, sometimes gruesome, in fact often gruesome. They became equated with slaughter of beast and men, reaching from Babylon to Mexico. The most gruesome events became connected to sacrifice. It was necessary that there should be teachers among men to change these practices gradually to a direction when sacrifice could become not merely outer, even shattering, events but where sacrifice could become more and more an inner event, a solemn decision of offering up inwardly or at least to accompany the outer sacrifice with an inner process. A feeling of inner awakening became important. It took a long time to learn this. It was not intended to lessen the sacrifice, make it less tangible but rather to bring sacrifice, the capacity to offer, within the measure of man. Perhaps the greatest teacher of antiquity, sent to prepare and to teach the inwardness of sacrifice was Melchizedek, the priest of the sun. He was to lead the understanding of the sun, of warmth within man, toward the time when the very being of the sun, the Christ himself, would descend and become a human being. This is shown to us by the fact that, when Melchizedek met with Abraham he, as the first one, celebrated the act of sacrifice of the sun, the sun giving himself to all things on earth, whether they be great or small. This process became the world image expressed in the Last Supper. There were many phases in between.

I want to recall the painting by Michelangelo of the creation of Adam. Something important was set into motion which should be kept in mind when we unroll before us the history of sacrifice. Through the finger of the Godhead Adam received the first touch of self-awareness. It is among the greatest gifts which human beings can receive to be individuals, to be themselves. They cannot learn to sacrifice without attaining this self-awareness. We find this element throughout history. In the very first sacrifice the Father God released his own son so that he may become independent. There are always two. Where we find the teaching of sacrifice, there are always at least two, right down to the "Last Supper." The disciple whom the Lord loves, John, had to be close, almost like his son, at his breast. We find a wonderful intermediary element depicted in the Greek statue of Hermes, or Mercury, by Praxiteles, who holds on his arm a child in the most tender way. The child is Dionysos, the bringer of the Ego. Mercury holds him on his left arm. The right arm is broken off and one wonders what he was holding because the child reaches out toward something Mercury-Hermes is holding. One has found in a description of the statue, when it was still whole, that the child, the Ego, is reaching out to grapes. We have to keep this in mind. There is always this element of teaching, the learning of the inner sacrifice, together with coming nearer to the bread and wine, that there are two: one who gives, who holds, who brings the promise, ultimately of the World-Ego. The promise of the—"I"—that is the same in each one of us. And the small individual ego, each one of us carries also in its precious singleness, and the urge and the longing for that which is the same for *every* human being.

From the first moment of Adam's birth there must be the giver and the taker. Without that the Ego cannot be and the sacrifice cannot be. There is a very essential aspect of this whole complex of sacrifice. This can be called the aspect of the lamb, of the sheep, of the shepherd, of all that has to do with Abel: a shepherd of sheep and of beings. The lamb, the ram, is found caught not on the ground where Abraham is willing to sacrifice Isaac, but on top of a tree, entangled by his horns. A lamb, was sacrificed, for thousands of years in Israel, as the Paschal lamb, and

in many other places too. There is, too, the Lamb of
God, to which John the Baptist points when the
Christ passes by him and his disciples. This whole
complex of the lamb, or ram, has two important aspects. Always, the lamb—ram was symbolized by its
two horns. You will know pictures of ordinary and also
highly bred rams which have these marvelous shell-
like horns, rolled into themselves and then sticking
out with one little twist. The two horns, innocent and
yet strong, have been known throughout the ages in
many cultures.

This played a great role on the mountain of Moriah, where Abraham was called to sacrifice. It was the
place where Melchizedek resided, who had his own
mystery place around which people gradually built a
city later known as Jerusalem. On Moriah the Temple
of Solomon was being built. One can still see today
this vast empty area in the midst of which now stands
a wonderful mosque, the Dome of the Rock, where
inside is shown the rock of the sacrifice which Abraham is supposed to have used for the offering of
Isaac. It is one of the holiest places for Mohammed-
ans, for Jews and for Christians alike. There also must
have stood the tree where the ram was caught with its
two horns.

The two-horned ram also seemed to be imprint-
ed into the being of Moses in many representations.
Moses has often been represented with two horns
springing from his forehead, as if he would be the
carrier of the power of the ram. These two horns are
the remnants of an organ of sight, an organ which
once beheld the gods. It was called and is being
called again today, the two-petalled lotus flower. It
radiated from the forehead of Moses as the last part

of this organ with which the godhead could be perceived by many people. This is the first aspect to be kept in mind with regard to the lamb. The lamb, the sheep, the pure beast, is in charge of the shepherd. It is the one who is offered at Paschal time and who carries, from out of the cosmos, the indication of the two-pronged organ for seeing the Gods.

The other aspect, closely related to it, is the place in the cosmos from which the lamb is coming. The lamb, or if you like, the ram, is part of the twelve great signs of the zodiac. I will quickly mention the twelve Zodiacal signs in the circle: crab, lion, virgin, scales, scorpio, sagittarius, capricorn, waterman, fishes, twins, bull, ram. The two-horned ram. If one relates these signs to the twelve senses of man we come to the five highest senses: waterman—warmth, fishes—hearing, twins—Ego, bull—thought, ram—sense of word. There are twice two pairs, standing opposite to each other, formed by warmth and the sense of ego, and by hearing and sense of thought. The sense of word has a central position in this whole configuration of influences streaming together from the cosmos. We all, as human beings, are open to it. We must keep in mind that something having to do with the sense of word is central in this particular region.

Thus, whether it is in speech, in language, in the perception of the Word—here seems to lie a key to the process of offering, of sacrifice. Human speech, however abused or empty it may have become, still inhabits a central place. One might say it is the altar on which we are meant to learn to celebrate. This is so for each speaking person, each person struggling for speech.

But the word, our very words, are also the greatest, the most precious riches we may have to offer. Even if they only consist of the two mites, the two pennies of the poor widow, they are of that precious gender of which sacrifices may be made.

The Divine Word became flesh and it sacrificed itself in the fullness of time. Ever since, at that holy place from which our own words emanate, the time prepares itself when—like a child most dear to us—a living Word will issue. Then offering will have become truly the most important deed of a true Man, of a full human being, one who will have achieved true humanity. Easter will have fulfilled itself.

Perpetual Easter

Easter Sunday, April 10, 1977, Beaver Run, PA

When from out the widths of worlds
The Sun speaks to the human senses
And joy from out the depths of soul
Unites itself with light in the beholding
Then from out of sheaths of selfhood
Thoughts move into distances of space
And dimly bind
Man's being with the Spirit.

Wenn aus den Weltenweiten
Die Sonne spricht zum Menschensinn
Und Freude aus den Seelentiefen
Dem Licht sich eint im Schauen,
Dann ziehen aus der Selbstheit Hulle
Gedanken in die Raumesfernen
Und binden dumpf
Des Menchen Wesen an des Geistes Sein.

This verse for Easter in the Calendar of the Soul[1] has guided me toward this long and imaginative attempt in our region to celebrate this Easter; to *attempt* to celebrate Easter. I was deeply moved by the radiance, seriousness and clarity of the wonderful service[2] this morning. I have seen the lovely colors of the "zodiacal eggs" that Peter has produced for us, with the help of Joanna and many others. I understand also that when one of the baskets with its 12 eggs was designated for my own use, concern was expressed that I should not overeat myself! and I am very grateful to be looked after in this way! Many other wonderful events have taken place: the performance of the Easter Saturday play in Copake; this morning the Easter Sunday play under the trees. I believe on Saturday evening there was a premiere in Kimberton Hills of an Easter morning scene by Joel.

On the evening of Easter Sunday one should not overlook a word that occurs in the Calendar of the Soul: the word joy—Freude, even though it is not easy, if one is honest, to feel satisfied with how far one has come in the understanding of this festival. At Easter we are powerfully aided by our environment. The onrush of new life, the new cycle of becoming, the glory of the green blade that everywhere arises, the red bud, the twitter of the birds: they all are engaged in the most wonderful way in a celebration of forthcoming. One is inclined in this annually renewed wonder to marvel at its strength and glory and to seek the Lord of the earth in these events. To hear ringing

---

1. "The Calender of the Soul" by Rudolf Steiner, Easter verse 1. The Anthroposophic Press, Spring Valley, 1974.
2. "The Festival of Youth," a Sunday celebration originating in Rudolf Steiner's work with the Waldorf Schools between 1919-1924.

in one's ears, perhaps from the Easter Sunday play, the ancient call of Hibernia, of the Lord of the Elements, is to begin to feel the first inkling of the realities of what it may mean: the cosmic force, the leader of the cosmic forces; the Cosmic Christ. And, yes, linked with this is joy!

We can ask ourselves: "How shall we be part of this new cycle of forthcoming which the world around us is celebrating? All around us this new beginning will sprout with immeasurable force into the relentless proliferating power of nature. There will be intimations of the relentless cycle of procreation, the mutual feeding upon each other, vast and powerful, pitiless, untamed, wild. It is beautiful, tremendous, but incomplete—incomplete without man, this ridiculous creature.

I have experienced that Easter is the hardest of all the existing festivals to celebrate truly. It is hard also to celebrate with children, in truth and honesty. One can dwell in beauty and joy for a certain while, but then one will be even more aware of the inner, solitary, gnawing feeling of inadequacy and the constant pointing toward the grave and to the stone upon the grave. It is perhaps not unimportant to experience the overall embracing consolation of resurrection out of which everything that is to be can alone hope to find its meaning. It must not come a moment too early if it shall be true for the human soul.

It must not come before the abundant experience of inconsolable pain inherent in the events that precede the perpetual Easter that has been now planted into the world through the Mystery of Golgotha. This awareness of pain must not be cheated. There must not be too early a rejoicing! Death lies before the resurrection. This morning, I experienced once again the beautiful words of the Festival of Youth. When I listened to these words I was very much aware not only of their relevance to those who were confirmed, but of their immense Easterly power. I would like to read them in a translation used for this service, part of John 17, which is often called the High Priestly Prayer and around which, one may feel, the whole service is grouped.

> "Father, the hour has come; reveal now to your Son—so that your Son may reveal of you—how you have given Him power over all flesh, that He may bestow eternal life on all those you gave Him to be His own. But this is eternal life, that they recognize you as the only true God and Jesus Christ as Him you sent.
>
> I have revealed you on earth to lead to its goal the work you laid upon me to do. And now reveal me, Father, with the revelation that became mine through you before the world yet existed. I have made you manifest for the human beings whom you—from out of the world—have given me to be my part. Yours they were and you gave them to me and they have remained filled with your word. So have they recognized how all you have given me came out of you. For the thought powers which you have given me I have brought to them. . . ."

"For the thought powers which you have given me I have brought to them." We, at Easter time, are given to think of Christianity, of Christ, in terms of the historic Mystery of Golgotha. We think of the landscape of Palestine, of the events described in various ways in the Gospels. We try to live through Holy Week and its events and we try on Good Friday to follow the more intimate and the rapidly intensifying events of what is called the Mystery of Golgotha, reaching from the deeds at the Last Supper—from the Washing of the Feet, the Breaking of Bread and Sharing of the Wine through to the Scourging, the Crowning with Thorns, the Carrying of the Cross—and then to the final consummation.

All this has its divine sense only if within its tremendous reality we can experience that every single aspect of the story has its unique nature, because for one world-historic moment and for one moment alone, the physical and the spiritual world were *one*. No nail that was used, no cup, no garment, was either only physical or only spiritually significant; they were both significant at the same time. All that took place and is described as history is at the same time written as into a scroll: World History of the Spirit *and* of Man.

We can rightly conceive of this as a historic event if we feel that all it describes is at the same time the Mysterium Magnum, the great mystery of the Incarnation, of the divine into the physical. It is incarnation of the Godhead in His passion, His crucifixion, His resurrection. The sense and purpose of man is contained in this becoming physical of the Spirit. But at the same time the Mysterium Magnum means something quite specific in an occult sense. It means the Three can be One and the One can be Three. That is the meaning, occultly, of the Mysterium Magnum.

In Beaver Run the friends turned to a very special kind of Easter experience, one that could be experienced through the Mysteries of Hibernia in Ireland. There, out of the most living, yet ancient spirit practices, it was possible, spiritually, to experience what took place, at the same time, physically over in Palestine. In Hibernia, parallel to, and even before it took place, one experienced this historic event purely spiritually.

This participation took place in a quite different way evoking Him who became flesh, who went through His passion, crucifixion and resurrection in Palestine. He was evoked not as incarnating into the flesh of Jesus, but as that part which is heralded to come in the clouds. He was experienced as the One—in the form of the One—who would again begin to be seen in our time in the clouds.

We have to ask ourselves then: shall we now look to the clouds? Shall we lift up our eyes to the clouds? And of course we must lift up our eyes to the clouds. What do we see when we look up—what may we see? I have just read, newly published in an anthroposophical journal, in excerpts, the following: "For 17 years now one has been able to develop the laser beam. It was immediately recognized that this laser beam which has 5,000 times more power than the light of the sun, would be best utilized for war purposes. One has now quite recently managed to solve the most difficult problem: namely so to reduce the technology of what amounts (expressed in old fashioned terms) to a ray gun, the technology required by the laser gun and which is to be utilized over vast distances; it is possible to reduce its size in such a way that it can be compacted into a package that could be below the approximate 60,000 lbs. which can be lifted into space and orbited, placed upon a space shuttle, and then from there be directed to any given space on the earth making the previous generation of weaponry, of rockets with atomic bombs, superfluous. The strength of this beam is such that it does not even matter so much whether one can aim it as accurately as previous weapons as it can vaporize every known material completely, on first impact."

It is expected that by 1982 these guns will be operable and a tremendous race is on to perfect similar things in the east. So, above the clouds you will have cosmic shuttle guns which will use rays of light to destroy. Probably another big demonstration in front of the White House will do little to change that. It is an awesome challenge which lies in the fact that rays of light should be used by us not for laser—but in our thinking, and I am concerned tonight with one part of the Three that can be One in the Mysterium Magnum, with thinking.

Easter, seen from whatever aspect, spiritual or historical-physical, is the high festival of the Ego of the world. It should be a pledge to the Ego of Man. We have to consider when we turn to thinking that it forms a parallel development to the ego. But the *development* of the ego (or the self if you like) is something quite different from the *experience* of the ego. These are two different things. Yet in this whole problem we are paralleling in our ego development microcosmically what as the event of Gods goes on macrocosmically and which culminated in the Mystery of Golgotha. It is imperative to speak about the ego from time to time because the ego is being undermined and attacked, denied in its existence on almost every side. The ego is being explained, or rather explained away, as a minimal, residual experience of purely mechanical processes of a nervous kind that can be stimulated by all manner of things and manipulated through influences corresponding to the values of groups. The ego is being attacked through what as a group-soul remnant is still living vividly in our time. Yet the ego can only exist through the assimilation of all experiences that it has as a conscious entity through thought.

I would like to recommend to you two lectures (and particularly the first) which Rudolf Steiner gave in Munich on the 4th and 7th December 1909 called "The Ego: The God Within And The God Of External Revelation." I would like to quote two paragraphs from this first lecture:

"In what way, however, do we grasp the "I"? Do we grasp the world at all through the anthroposophical view? This anthroposophical view of the world arises in the most individual way, and is, at the same time, the most un-individual thing that can be conceived. It can only arise in the most individual way by the secrets of the cosmos revealing themselves in a human soul, into which stream the great spiritual beings of the world. And so the content of the world must be experienced in the human individuality in the most individual way, but at the same time, it must be experienced with a character of complete impersonality. Whoever will experience the true character of cosmic mysteries must stand entirely on the standpoint from which he says: Whoever still heeds his own opinion, cannot come to Truth. That is indeed the peculiar ("eigenartige") nature of anthroposophical truth that the observer may have no opinion of his own, no preference for this or the other theory, that he may not love this or the other view more than any other because of his own special individual qualities. As long as he stands on this standpoint, it is impossible for the true secrets of the world to reveal themselves to him. He must pursue knowledge quite individually, but his individuality must develop so far, that it no longer has anything personal, i.e. anything of his own peculiar sympathies and antipathies. This must be taken strictly and earnestly. Whoever still has any preference for these or the other ideas and views, whoever can incline to this or the other because of his education or temperament, will never recognize objective truth"[1].

And then a little later in direct relationship to our subject: "One must strongly emphasize that in our time it is impossible for independent spiritual knowledge to decide through any special preference for either the Oriental or the Occidental view of the world. Whoever says according to his different temperament he prefers the nature, the laws of the world as existing in the Oriental or correspondingly in the Occidental view, has not yet a full understanding for what is here essential. One should not decide, e.g., for the greater

---

1. "The Universal Human," Rudolf Steiner, Collection of Lectures, 1909, 1910. Anthroposophic Press, 1990.

significance of, let us say, the Christ, as compared with what Oriental teaching recognizes, because one inclines to the Christ through one's Occidental education or one's temperament. One is only fitted to answer the question "How is the Christ related to the Orient?" when from a personal standpoint the Christian is as indifferent to one as the Oriental. As long as one has preference for this or the other, so long is one unsuited to make a decision. One first begins to be objective when one lets the facts alone speak, when one heeds no reasons derived from personal opinion, but lets facts alone speak in this sphere"[1].

In this relationship the immediate question that arises is: how can one make these facts speak without one's opinion? Only in this sense can the world proportion of the Christ event be understood without magnifying it beyond permission through mere belief. We have to remind ourselves that we must try to pursue what we pursue in such a way that it is gained individually though it has only validity to the extent that one's individuality has been overcome *at the same time*. This is the ego's task and cannot be performed by anything else. It is even impossible to imagine this situation with the forces of the most refined astrality. Only the ego experiencing itself can have a first inkling of what this means. This ego task is something else than merely a "psychological event" that goes on. Wherever it occurs there is the perpetual inner Easter of man.

We may ask further: how is it that we experience this already as little children? How do we gain experiences of this true arena of our consciousness? Rudolf

---

1. Ibid—pg. 37.

Steiner, in lectures called "Life Between Death and Rebirth"[1] says: "A simple observation can convince everyone how ego-consciousness develops and becomes strong in a child. Suppose he knocks his head against the corner of a table. If you observe closely you will find that the feeling of "I" is intensified after such a thing happens. In other words, the child becomes aware of himself, is brought nearer to a knowledge of self. Of course, it need not always amount to an actual injury or scratch. Even when the child puts his hand on something there is an impact on a small scale that makes him aware of himself. You will have to conclude that a child would never develop ego-consciousness if resistance from the world outside did not make him aware of himself. The fact that there is a world external to himself makes possible the unfolding of ego-consciousness, the consciousness of the "I." At a certain point in his life this consciousness of the "I" dawns in the child, but what has been going on up to this point does not come to an end. It is simply that the process is reversed. The child has developed ego-consciousness by becoming aware that there are objects outside himself. In other words, he separates himself from them. Once this ego-consciousness has developed it continues to come in contact with things. Indeed it must do so perpetually. Where do the impacts take place? An entity that contacts nothing can have no knowledge of itself, not, at least, in the world in which we live! The fact is that from the moment ego-consciousness arises, the "I" impacts

---

1. "Life Between Death and Rebirth" 16 Lectures, 1912/1913. Anthroposophic Press, New York, 1968. Lecture 3—"Man's Journey Through the Planetary Spheres and the Significance of a Knowledge of Christ," November 18, 1912.

upon its own inner corporeality, begins to impact upon its own body inwardly. To picture this you need only think of a child waking up every morning. The ego and the astral body pass into the physical and etheric bodies and the ego impacts upon them. Now, even if you only dip your hand in water and move it along, there is resistance wherever your hand is in contact with the water. It is the same when the ego dives down in the morning and finds its own inner life playing around it. During the whole of life the ego is within the physical and etheric bodies and impacts upon them on all sides, just as when you splash your hand in water you become aware of your hand on all sides. When the ego plunges down into the etheric body and the physical body it comes up against resistance everywhere, and this continues through the whole of life. Throughout his life the man must plunge down into his physical and etheric bodies every time he wakes. Because of this, continual impacts take place between the physical and etheric bodies on the one side and the ego and astral body on the other. The consequence is that the entities involved in the impact are worn away—ego and astral body on the one side, physical and etheric bodies on the other. Exactly the same thing happens as when there is continual pressure between two objects. They wear each other away. This is the process of aging, of becoming worn out, that sets in during the course of man's life, and it is also the reason why he dies as a physical being."

With the adult that is no longer required although it is still there, though more inwardly. We have our collisions consciously every moment we wake within our inner self, with our interior experi-

ences. "Just think of it. If we had no physical body, no
etheric body, we could not maintain our ego-consciousness. True, we might be able to unfold such
consciousness, but we could not maintain it. To do
this we must always be impacting our own inner constitution. The consequence of this is the extraordinarily important fact that the development of our ego
is made possible by destroying our own being. If there
were no impact between the members of our being,
we could have no ego-consciousness. When the question is asked, "What is the purpose of destruction, of
aging, of death?" the answer must be that it is in order
that man may evolve, that ego-consciousness may develop to further stages. If we could not die, that is the
radical form of the process, we could not be truly
"man"[1].

This awareness of self through death belongs to
the perpetual Easter. But what is described here, still
comparatively crudely as an experience and yet of immense importance, has yet a much finer micro-cos-
mic process that corresponds to it. This is the process
with which we in our ego awareness enter into life as
human beings through our thinking capacity. This
capacity, by which we are meant to become the crown
of worlds, has to add itself to every single thing
around us to give it sense, meaning and purpose. It is
that process through which we are not only creatures,
part of the relentless wheel of life, but creators. The
activity of thought undergoes that process also that
we as a matter of nature undergo in the acquisition of
our ego consciousness by virtue of constant collisions
with the world around and with the world within us.

---

1. Ibid—Pg. 34-36 (Carlo's free rendering of English translation).

How does that take place? Our thought life, in as much as it is permeated by our ego, is the arena of our constantly renewed inner Easter. It contains in rapidity that which is taking place over long stretches of time and which was significantly, centrally and archetypically enacted at the Mystery of Golgotha. It contains the seven steps of what is called the Christian Initiation. For thought process can, and often does, take place in this way.

We take hold of the content, the subject. If we can bring to it that element which alone makes us part of the Christian development of the world we will bring to it love, warmth. Awareness of warmth which we ascribe to the subject makes the process I am describing relevant. Other ways of thinking do not contain it. Most of our thinking does not contain it. But it *can* contain it. It means taking hold of the subject, the content, with love. Taking hold of the subject with love means that the process described takes slightly longer, is slightly more deliberate than other thought processes which take place in us automatically.

The first part of this "bending down" toward the subject, corresponds to the Washing of the Feet, whether it concerns a stone, plant, animal or a human being or complicated substructures of these. To take hold of the subject in the attitude of the Washing of the Feet, initiates the further seven steps of this thought process. It is followed by the puzzlement and pain of questioning—"die Fragepein." It is followed by the repeated experience of the desperate struggle to understand. We can like the content, we can try to love the subject, we can try to hold it in reverence but we may not yet understand it. This corresponds to the feeling of Scourging. The third step is to pass through the next phase of holding it in mind, in reverence, in pain, and that is to seek to understand it with one's spirit. All around one is assailed by mockery, maligned, unaided, lonely. It is the most painful of the first three steps and it corresponds to that which in the Christian Initiation is called the Crowning with Thorns. The fourth is, despite everything, to carry it forth, hold it fast, carry it perhaps for days, for weeks, for months or for years. It corresponds to the Carrying of the Cross. And then comes the moment when the thought which until then has lived in concepts, expressible in language—dies.

Immediately it seems to glide from there into the next phase. It descends into doubt, into all kinds of feelings that want to turn away from it and in which in particular we become aware of *ourselves* in the process as a central actor. We become aware of the inadequacy of thinking. It is as if the first steps: The Washing of the Feet, the Scourging, the Crowning with Thorns, the dying away of the words as we knew them would be an affirmation that thinking leads to nothing! That is the Descent into Hell. If the curtain will be rent in twain at that moment, then, in the seventh step, we may be able to think the thought *without* our brain. Where that has taken place, the thinking of a thought without our brain, the Resurrection has taken place, the Ascent. We became aware that we are now no longer thinking concepts, thought-ideas, word proliferations in chains of logic—but *seeds* from which indeed the green blade rises.

Many of us have had this experience many times, only our attention has been inadequate to perceive it. It is perhaps the innermost activity of the ego. It is, in intimate detail, an experience of going through death within which is the renewal of life. It is the most quick-ening, most self-revealing ego activity of which man is capable and the wonder of it consists in the following: the steps that lead towards the dying of the thought are totally unmistakable for a close and unprejudiced factual inner observation of oneself. This thought life that dies away is constantly repeated by him who strives spiritually; except usually he is not yet suffi-ciently aware. This process carries within itself a little death, all the time. It is that kind of death, that kind of collision, that takes place spiritually, not physically. It is the kind of collision which occurs every time when, as Rudolf Steiner once called it, we have learned, just as we stretch our hands to touch something physically, we stretch out our will with our thought. Every time we do that a collision takes place, a little death occurs. In this little death there is always present the evidence of resurrection. It lies in the power of the co-creative ego, a power received through something that can be de-scribed. It is the same which we are meant to experi-ence as Easter in our time as spiritually striving human beings. We may begin to feel it in the words: In Christo Morimur—in Christ we die. In this word there lives the seed of life. We must learn to become aware that to die in Christ, with Christ, means: to participate through Him in Spirit-life. This can be inwardly expe-rienced when we time and again dwell upon the words: In Christo Morimur, by gradually feeling with-in ourselves the reality of that power which He brought through His incarnation: the power of love. As we repeat to ourselves: In Christo Morimur, we feel: we love the Son.

Exactly the same takes place in our thinking. Out of the motherground of wisdom which guides our thinking, we accompany with our experience of loss, the Passion and Scourging and Crowning and Crucifixion, and the certainty that the Son is born. This Son are *we* ourselves, in our *new* thought. This Son, out of the dying thought, this thought that "I" no longer as individual think although it is my innermost achievement, is World thought. It is thought power that exists out of, and is permeated by, love.

This, I would suggest, is one of the constant Easter experiences, the perpetual Easter. This experience is neither only the history of what took place in Palestine nor the history of the Mysteries of Hibernia. Yet both are contained in the ever-renewed Mystery of the Ego in its struggle to be part of the Three in One, in that part where it lives as thinking. Where the Christ is experienced in the words: In Christo Morimur, we learn to add the reality of our experience: We love the Christ—we love the Son. Easter becomes a festival which once a year should focus all our imaginary powers and capacities to recollect and worship, so that Easter also becomes an experience of our everyday existence, for there it also occurs— when we, with Easter powers, think.

LECTURE FOURTEEN

Excerpts from a Whitsun Address

May 29, 1979, Beaver Run, PA

Dear friends,
Rudolf Steiner spoke a great deal about Whitsun.
For many years he spoke about it. In 1910 he spoke
about Spiritual Science as a Whitsun gift. He spoke in
the course of the years again and again about Whitsun. And he did so also at the last Whitsun at which
he was able to speak, on June 8, 1924. By that time he
was at work in Breslau for the tremendous series of activities that ranged from the Agricultural Course and
meetings with the young people and Class Lessons
culminating on June 18, with his visit to the Lauen-
stein, the first home for curative education. There he
gave his astonishing agreement to offer a course of
lectures on curative education. This, as you know, began one day after St. John, on the 25th of June, in
Dornach. The inception of this last Whitsun festival is
surrounded by the Karma lectures, by this enormous
stream, this outpouring of the many, many karma lectures, both in Switzerland and in Germany, even in

Prague and then in England. Set into this stream, which is almost impossible to gather up in one's mind, on the 4th of June, just before he left for the Whitsun activities, he gave a very remarkable lecture. It is remarkable in consideration of what we have now before us. On Whitsunday, the 8th, during the sequence of the karma lectures, he spoke on the seven planetary spheres, characterizing them anew, for he had done so before, also at a Whitsun, several years earlier. In the "Last Address," in September of that year, on hand of the personality of Raphael-Novalis, he spoke about the seven planetary spheres again: the seven planetary spheres through which we all pass in the life after death. Of these he spoke in a new way on Whitsunday. He also once more characterized the long time that is spent by our eternal part which we have been able to carry through this cleansing process, passing through the spheres of Moon, Mercury and Venus. He mentions that a reflection of the period which takes place on the spirit-sun falls between the 21st and the 42nd year of our earthly lives.

On June 4th he gave a lecture entitled: "The Whitsun-thought as a Foundation for the Right Feeling Toward an Understanding of Karma"[1]. The Whitsun-thought as a foundation for the right feeling toward an understanding of Karma! It is a magnificent lecture and seems like a festival within Rudolf Steiner's lectures. It is sparkling and radiating in the very words which he uses, making bold new word formations to express what is so difficult to express in the translation from spirit reality into earthly language.

---

1. The Whitsun Festival. Its place in the Study of Karma." Dornach, 4th June, 1924. 1945 Anthroposophic Press, New York (c) H. Collison.

In this very full and wonderful lecture there are a few things that we can pluck from the marvelous sound of his utterance and use for our purposes.

There are three very important steps he makes and they are truly *important.* I became aware of their importance, for a similar motif occurs at two or three other Whitsun lectures at different times. When we are born into earth existence we are born into the world of space. That is the heritage and the justified inheritance of earthly man, of the earthly child, to find himself in the spatial world and to learn to be able to move freely within it, and within it to experience himself in this threefold direction that space endows upon all its inhabitants. This is linked to the act of creation, to the spiritual power of creation, leading the spirit into substance. We belong to it as human beings, entering from the spheres of our real origin into the conditions of space. This belongs to the creative act of the forces of the Father: Ex Deo Nascimur. Out of God we are born. To that is attached one of the holiest possibilities of our experience, a moment that we can perceive and experience at Christmas, when the birth of the human child out of spirit heights carries within it the wonder of this creative act. This holy act of human inheritance, to move freely in space and not to be deprived of it, characterizes the essential aspect of the early Kaspar Hauser tragedy: to be deprived from moving in space.

Rudolf Steiner describes how, as we experience ourselves in this world of space, we must become aware of the fact that everything in it is impinged upon by a different quality that is only a stranger in space and yet determines all life. That quality is Time. Everything originates at a certain moment, passes through a state of development and evolution in order to pass out again—from birth to death. The element of time is not at home in space. It lives and dwells in it as a visitor affecting all existence. It originates from a place in the cosmos we call the sun. From a source that is less than anything the human being can conceive as matter, infinite possibilities of the spirit world stream into space as time. The sun becomes the originator of time within space. To this belongs, including the mystery of death, that man as a being born on earth has inherited the words: In Christo morimur. In Christ we die,—because the being of the sun that is in this way the creator and originator of Time is the Being of Christ. It is conceivable to experience the important discovery when men began to discover evolution as a process in time; and with it the evolution of the human gender in evolution. All evolution and development went together with this milestone. At the same time one can sense that there are usurpers of this stream of time. The usurpers of evolution begin to play a new part in the consciousness of man, for instance, the one who appeared as the so called "False Czar", Demetrius, in the 17th Century.

Finally, Rudolf Steiner speaks about the bridge that extends forever between earth and cosmos, reaching from the Ex Deo Nascimur to the In Christo Morimur. I would like to quote from his lecture: "Imagine that man would not only encapsule himself and his experiences within the world of space but would accept Christ into himself, who has come out of the world of time into the world of space; who himself has brought *time* into the spaces of the earth. Through this he overcomes, in death, death itself. Ex Deo Nascimur, In Christo Morimur. But Christ brings the message that when space is overcome, if one has started to get to know the sun as the creator of time beyond space, when one feels oneself within the sun, then the physical disappears and the etheric and the astral appear. But now the etheric begins to live spiritually, not as the blue of the sky as we beheld it before but as a light-redness shining into the whole cosmos. And out of this light-redness not only shine the stars but the stars touch us now with the effects of their love. And man can feel if he now places himself imaginatively into all this, as standing upon the earth, having left the physical behind, the etheric permeating and radiating toward him this lilac red, and the stars not as shining points but as rays of love, like the caressing of human love. As one feels this divine element within one self, as one feels this divine world fire as ones true being, feeling oneself in the etheric world-all, experiencing the expressions of the spirit in the astral shining of the worlds then it creates the inner experience of spirit radiance. Christ told this to the apostles. They had permeated themselves long enough with this thought and when they felt the effect of it in themselves, it appeared to them like the fiery tongues of Whitsun. Then they felt the dying, the falling away of the physical upon the earth, but at the same time they felt: this is not death, but for the physical of the earth there now arises the Spirit-Self, the Manas of the Universe: Per Spiritum Sanctum Reviviscimus"[1]. To the holy spirit we arise, we divine it[2].

This is one paragraph of this lecture, from 4th June, 1924, in Dornach. Before I return to this lecture

---

1. See above.
2. English translation of PSSR by Pietzner.

for another small paragraph, I would like to picture
what is described. A vessel is described that consists of
the three festivals—of Christmas with the E.D.N., of
Easter with the I.C.M., and of Whitsun with the
P.S.S.R. A vessel, roughly half of the year. This one
half of the year carries these three festivals. The question now arises about the other half of the year. Let us
now return for a moment to Rudolf Steiner. He says:
"Thus one can look toward the threefoldness of one
half of the year. Christmas-thought: E.D.N., Easter-
thought: I.C.M., Whitsun-thought: P.S.S.R. And now
remains the other half of the year. If one understands
it in such a way then there opens up for the human
being also the other side of this life. One must understand the relationship of the physical to the soul existence of man and to the supra-physical. It combines
the freedom through which the human being partic-
ipates on earth in the spirit. Then one also understands the relationship between Christmas, Easter
and Whitsun as the festival of the free human being
on earth. If one understands this through these three
thoughts and then feels called upon to understand
the remainder of the year, there arises the other half
of human life. I have indicated this to you by saying:
then one looks at human destiny, at Karma, and behind it there appear all the hierarchies, the work and
the weaving of the hierarchies. Therefore it is so great
to look truly into a human destiny, because behind it
appear all the hierarchies"[1].

Thus one can see the festivals along these lines: a
vessel that extends from Christmas to Easter to Whitsun like the sickle of the moon and in it the other half

1. See above lecture reference.

of the year—not yet visible. This invisible sun rests in the chalice of the moon; the visible half is irradiated by an as yet unknown Michaelmas, floating as it were in the cup that consists of the three Rosicrucian words, E.D.N., I.C.M., P.S.S.R. In this rests the promise of Michaelmas, the promise of the Michaelmas festival of which Rudolf Steiner expected that we would find its reality. He himself would not lend a hand in bringing it about, until we would be ready for it. This Michaelmas festival, resting in the half moon or vessel of the first half of the year is illuminated by the knowledge of Karma and Reincarnation. This is also the promise of the new Christianity.

I experience this circle of festivals so that one can sometimes feel it like a ring, hovering above us, or sometimes rising above us like a lens, a cosmic lens between ourselves and the spiritual world. As each lens has a focus so too this lens has a focus. This year the focus will be at St. John's time, the St. John's festival; Midsummer reaching into August. It is the time in which the garment of Michael is being woven. It is the time in which from the earth, both from its matter as well as from the human beings and their activities, there reach up into the spirit threads of spirit silver, reaching into the heights at St. John's time toward the activity of the Archangel Uriel. There, the silver is changed into gold, to spirit gold, and becomes the garment of Michael. Some part of this cloth of gold would have to be woven by those who want to give an offering at Michaelmas. And this garment, in as much as it can be woven together with all the forces of the earth into the cosmos this summer, is a sign of the reality of our preparedness concerning the spiritual world.

In the ten days that extend from Ascension to Whitsun we can be aware of something which one can never be quite aware of with the same depth and intensity at any other time of the year. It is akin to the much greater and deeper awareness and experience which the Apostles had during those ten days. It is the experience of our limitations, of our loneliness, of our feeling of having been abandoned, particularly by ourselves and our good spirit. It is the experience of being forsaken, confused and utterly fragile and vulnerable. We may experience this to the profoundest extent to which we may be capable, yet must not show the slightest sign of it to anybody else, imposing no burden upon the soul experience of anybody else!

To learn in the ten days to be alone and to stand on one's own feet without any comfort, without any reassurance, without any encouragement, I believe, helps Whitsun to become real. The feeling of the P.S.S.R. would seal this vessel, complete it, round it, so that it carries within it the being of St. John's time, preparing for it. Through the spirit, the Holy Spirit, we would arise.

And yet, dear friends, if we only would take it quite, quite real! This tremendous, divine thing that is contained in the words—Holy Spirit—is, I believe, always with us, for it is the spirit that makes us into general human beings. And if anything has grown visibly and tangibly in this world certainly for the last 100 years since the new Michael age has begun, it is that we can recognize all over the world that men have become aware how this uniting Spirit lives, or can live, within us. It is not the spirit of nationalities, not that which has separated us and separates us again and again most grievously and most stupidly from one another; not Englishmen and Frenchmen and Americans and Germans, also not Camphillians or any other group existence. But the spirit in which man recognizes himself as a part of mankind—that belongs to the power of the Holy Spirit through which we arise. It is that Spirit with the consequences of which the being of Michael can live, work, and be.

It is my hope that perhaps at St. John's time there will be a certain amount of silver woven into the gold and that we will prepare for the other half of the year where the hierarchies may guide our insight and ac- knowledgment of Karma towards the time of Michael- mas.